I wish to thank the following people who were of great assistance in the preparation of this book: Katherine Keena, Mary Levey, and Mary Degenhardt of the Girl Scouts of the U.S.A.; Elizabeth Shenton, Assistant to the Director, the Arthur and Elizabeth Schlesinger Library on the History of Women in America, Radcliffe College; Ilene Ielmini, the Georgia Historical Society at Savannah; Ann Valdez, Native American Education Services College, American Indian Center, Chicago, Illinois; Jack Hicks and Rick Bean, Deerfield Public Library, Deerfield, Illinois; Natalie Rothbart; Peggy Rogers; and Leonard J. Brown.

I also consulted the Library of Congress, Washington, D.C.; the Smithsonian Institution, Washington, D.C.; the Chicago Historical Society; and the Southern Historical College Collection at the University of North Carolina at Chapel Hill, North Carolina.

These books and articles were especially helpful:

Addington, Sarah. "The First Girl Scout." *Good Housekeeping*, February 1927.

Choate, Anne Hyde, and Helen Ferris, eds. *Juliette Low and the Girl Scouts.* New York: Girl Scouts of the U.S.A., 1928.

Dictionary of American Biography, under the entry "Low, Juliette Gordon."

Gordon, Arthur. "I Remember Aunt Daisy." *Readers Digest*, March 1956, 120-122.

Lyon, Nancy. "Juliette Low: The Eccentric Who Founded the Girl Scouts." *Ms.*, November 1981.

McBride, Mary M. "Portrait of Juliette Low." *Good Housekeeping*, March 1933.

Notable American Women, 1607-1950, under the entry "Low, Juliette Gordon."

Price, Mrs. Theodore H. "Girl Scouts." *Outlook*, March 1918, 366-367.

Saxton, Martha. "The Best Girl Scout of Them All." *American Heritage*, June-July 1982, 38-47.

Schriner, Gertrude, and Margaret Rogers. *Daisy's Chicago Heritage*. Elk Grove, Ill.: Prairie Girl Scout Council, Inc., 1989.

Schultz, Gladys Denny, and Daisy Gordon Lawrence. *Lady from Savannah*. Philadelphia and New York: J.B. Lippincott Company, 1958.

United States Bureau of Education Bulletin, 1919, under the entry "Girl Scouts as an educational force."

Fern G. Brown

DAISY

and the Girl Scouts:

The Story of Juliette Gordon Low

Fern G. Brown
Illustrations by Marie DeJohn

Albert Whitman & Company
Morton Grove, Illinois

To my husband, Leonard,
and to our children, who have raised their
children to be good scouts.

Text copyright © 1996 by Fern G. Brown.
Illustrations copyright © 1996 by Marie DeJohn.
Published in 1996 by Albert Whitman & Company,
6340 Oakton Street, Morton Grove, Illinois 60053-2723.
Published simultaneously in Canada by Fitzhenry & Whiteside, Markham, Ontario.
Printed in the United States of America.
10 9 8 7 6 5 4

Picture credits

The cover and illustrations on pages 1, 21, 38, 58, 78, and 89 are by Marie DeJohn.

The photographs on pages I, III, V, VI, VII, and VIII of the photo insert section are
courtesy of the Girl Scouts of the U.S.A.

The photograph on page II is courtesy of the Smithsonian Institution.

Library of Congress Cataloging-in-Publication Data

Brown, Fern G.
    Daisy and the Girl Scouts: the story of Juliette Gordon Low / Fern Brown;
illustrated by Marie DeJohn.
            112p.   cm.
    Summary: Describes the vigorous and unconventional life of the founder of the
Girl Scout movement in the United States.
        ISBN 0-8075-1440-3 (hardcover)
        ISBN 0-8075-1441-1 (paperback)
        1. Low, Juliette Gordon, 1860-1927—Juvenile literature. 2. Girl Scouts of the
United States of America—Biography—Juvenile literature. 3. Girl Scouts—United States—
Biography—Juvenile literature. [1. Low, Juliette Gordon, 1860-1927. 2. Girl Scouts of the
United States of America—Biography.] I. DeJohn, Marie, ill.
II. Title.
HS3268.2.L68B76 1996
369.463'092—dc20   90-42360
[B]   CIP
[96]   AC

Contents

The Promise

ON MY HONOR, I WILL TRY:
   to serve God and my country,
   to help people at all times,
   and to live by the
   Girl Scout Law.

The Laws

I WILL DO MY BEST:
   to be honest
   to be fair
   to help when I am needed
   to be cheerful
   to be friendly and considerate
   to be a sister to every Girl Scout
   to respect authority
   to use resources wisely
   to protect and improve the
      world around me
   to show respect for myself
      and others through
      my words and actions.

Chapter One

Daisy, the Young Rebel

Her real name was Juliette Gordon Low, but everyone called her Daisy. When she was a young woman, fun-loving Daisy spent much of her time giving parties or being entertained. Her interest in anything never lasted long, and she flitted from one project to another. Although her friends found her charming, others thought she was odd and undependable.

Imagine everyone's surprise when, at age fifty-two, Daisy Low founded the Girl Scouts of the U.S.A.! Who would have thought that scatter-brained Daisy, who had health problems and could barely hear, would begin with two small troops and build an international organization? Yet she did. With enthusiasm, hard work, and much of her own money, Daisy proved she could do whatever she made up her mind to do.

Born on October 31, 1860, in Savannah, Georgia, Juliette Magill Kinzie Gordon was the second child of Eleanor Lytle Kinzie Gordon and William Washington Gordon II. Almost everyone in the Gordon family had a nickname. So when an uncle said, "I'll bet she'll be a daisy," Juliette was nicknamed Daisy.

About six months after Daisy was born, the Civil War began in the United States. The war was a struggle between the Northern states and the Southern states. Each region had different customs and different ways of thinking. Many people in the North wanted to abolish slavery, but most Southerners believed people should be able to own slaves. Some states felt state governments should be more powerful than the federal government. Other states disagreed. Then Abraham Lincoln was elected president, and the North gained control of the government. Several Southern states decided to leave the Union and form their own confederation of states. Mr. Lincoln didn't want the Southern states to leave the Union. In December 1860, South Carolina seceded, or broke away, from the rest of the United States. On April 12, 1861, fighting broke out in Charleston, South Carolina, between the Confederates or "Rebels" from the Southern states and the Union army or "Yankees " from the North.

Daisy's paternal grandfather, the first William Washington Gordon, had been a Southerner. With a group of men he had built the Central of Georgia Railroad, and he had been mayor of Savannah several times. His son, Daisy's father, who was also named William Washington, was a partner in a cotton business and owned slaves. He became an officer in the Confederate army.

Daisy's mother was a Yankee. She had grown up in Chicago, which was in the North. Daisy's great-grandfather, John Kinzie, had been an Indian agent. He represented the U.S. government in dealing with Native Americans. John Kinzie married Eleanor Lytle McKillip, a widow with a daughter. In 1779, when she was nine years old, little Eleanor had been captured by a group of Seneca, who were part of the Iroquois Nation. She lived with them as Chief Cornplanter's daughter for four years. She dressed as a Native American and learned their language and customs. The Seneca treated her like a princess, and because she moved so fast, they named her "Little-Ship-Under-Full-Sail." Eleanor grew to love her Seneca family.

Eleanor's parents never stopped trying to get their daughter back. They asked Col. Guy Johnson, a British Indian agent, to help them. He went to Cornplanter's village and persuaded the chief to bring Eleanor to the next Council Fire so her parents could see her.

Eleanor was then thirteen. She had promised Chief Cornplanter that she would never leave the Seneca without his permission. But when she saw her mother, Eleanor ran into her outstretched arms. Seeing Eleanor with her mother made Chief Cornplanter decide that she belonged with her family, so he left her with them and went home. All her life Eleanor thought of Chief Cornplanter with great affection.

John and Eleanor Kinzie lived in a house near the Chicago River, the first built in the area that later became Chicago. Their son, John Harris Kinzie, born in 1803, also became a respected trader and friend of the Native Americans. Although there had been no school for John to attend, he spoke thirteen Native American dialects. He married Juliette Magill, a highly educated young woman from New York. She knew Latin and French, read Spanish and Italian, and later learned German.

Juliette Magill Kinzie loved adventure, and she was delighted when her husband was appointed sub-Indian agent at Fort Winnebago, at Portage, Wisconsin. In September 1830, they set out from Detroit for a wilderness life in Portage. The next March, after a grueling trip, they visited Chicago, where Mrs. Kinzie met her husband's relatives. She wrote down their accounts of early Chicago and the story of her mother-in-law's girlhood adventure as "Little-Ship-Under-Full-Sail." Later, Mrs. Kinzie made all her sketches and notes into a book, which included stories of her life as the wife of an Indian agent. It was called *Wau-bun*, which means "little dawn" in Potawatomi, and it was a great success. Later, Juliette Magill Kinzie wrote other books. Juliette Magill Kinzie Gordon–Daisy–was named for this intelligent and interesting grandmother.

Soon John Harris Kinzie resigned his position at Fort Winnebago and moved back to his boyhood home, where Chicago is now. He was made a full Indian agent. When his wife joined him in 1834, about fifty white people lived in the little town. A daughter was born to John and Juliette in 1835, and she was baptized in Chicago's first church. She was named Eleanor Lytle Kinzie for her grandmother. Eleanor, or Nellie, was Daisy's mother.

By 1837, the John Harris Kinzies were happily settled in their new brick home at the corner of Cass and

Michigan Streets. The village of Chicago was incorporated, and John Harris Kinzie was made the first president. As one of the founding families of Chicago, the Kinzies knew many important people. When Nellie was a child she was taken to the White House to meet President Zachary Taylor.

Nellie Kinzie was somewhat spoiled, but she was also charming, a fast thinker, and full of fun. She grew to be a lovely young woman who was extremely outgoing. Nellie met a schoolmate's brother, William Gordon, at Yale University where he was a student. When they met, he was dazzled by Nellie's funny stories and her lively personality. But to Nellie, William seemed shy and bashful. Then one morning, Nellie slid down a bannister in the Yale library, bumped into William Gordon at the foot, and flattened his hat. That day Nellie discovered he was not as shy as she had thought, and he fell fast in love with her. By the time William graduated from Yale, she, too, was in love.

William and Nellie were married on December 21, 1857. The newlyweds went to Savannah to live in the "Gordon House," on the corner of Bull and Oglethorpe, with William's widowed mother.

So although Nellie Kinzie Gordon and her family were from the North, she now lived in the South. The war put her in a delicate position. Her husband was a Confederate officer, but her brothers were in the Union army. Her beloved uncle, David Hunter, was the Union general responsible for bombing Fort Pulaski outside the city of Savannah. He was also a staunch abolitionist.

When Daisy was very young, food was scarce, and there was no money to buy new clothes. All the food and money that could be spared went to the Confederate soldiers. Little Daisy barely saw her father, but she was proud of him. When he came home, he'd stay a few days and then go back to the war. Daisy thought of the Yankees as the enemy. She wanted the fighting to stop before her papa was killed.

As the war went on, the South began to lose. In July 1864, because of the advancing Union army, so many aunts, cousins, friends—refugees from war-torn northern Georgia and Virginia—had left their homes and crowded into Grandmother Gordon's house that Daisy's mother moved her three daughters into a four-room cottage just outside of Savannah. In late fall, however, the Union army was so close that they had to move back to the big house to be under the protection of the city of Savannah.

By December 21, 1864, the Union army had marched from Atlanta to Savannah, and the mayor had met the Union forces outside the city to surrender. Daisy was then a lively four-year-old. She was small, with large, dark eyes and long, light brown hair. Her sister Eleanor, nicknamed Nelly, was six, and baby Alice was a year and a half. The little girls were thin and pale, and they had broken out in boils because they didn't have enough good food.

Soon after the surrender, Daisy and Nelly were playing in the parlor when they heard the sound of tramping boots. They climbed on chairs and peeked through the shutters. General Sherman's army! They watched, wide-eyed, as real live Yankees in blue uniforms marched past. The men were singing "When This Cruel War Is Over," a favorite song of both the North and South. Nelly and Daisy were highly indignant to hear the enemy sing a song their mother loved, and Daisy angrily refused to look at the Union army anymore.

A few evenings later, the maid flung open the Gordons' parlor door and announced, "General Sherman!" The Yankee general had brought letters from Daisy's grandparents in Chicago!

Daisy had heard General Sherman called "the Devil," so she expected him to have horns and a tail. Imagine her surprise to find that the hated Yankee general looked like any other man. General Sherman took Daisy on his lap. With an arm around Nelly, he told the little girls funny stories, and before long he had them laughing. He gave them a treat—rock sugar candy, made with real sugar. Sugar was not available in wartime Savannah, so this was the first time Nelly and Daisy had ever tasted it.

Later that week, another Yankee, General Howard, called on Daisy's mother. General Howard had only one arm. Even as a young child, Daisy was curious and asked a lot of questions.

"How did you lose your arm?" she asked the general.

"It was shot off in battle," he said.

Daisy asked if the Yankees had shot it off.

"No," he replied, "the Rebels."

"Did they!" exclaimed Daisy proudly. "Well, I s'pose my papa did it. He has shot lots of Yankees!"

Although the general didn't seem to be offended, Mrs. Gordon hurried her daughter from the room.

After the surrender, the families of Confederate officers were required to leave Savannah. General Sherman arranged for safe passage across enemy lines for the Gordons. Daisy's mother had decided to take her children to her parents' home in Chicago where they would be safe. Grandmother Gordon left her house and went to Etowah Cliffs, in northern Georgia, to stay with relatives.

In January 1865, Mrs. Gordon and her three little girls took a steamer headed to New York. It was a long, hard voyage, but Daisy didn't get seasick. When they docked, they were met by Mrs. Gordon's brothers, Arthur and George, who had come to escort them. The train from New York to Chicago was dirty and slow. The family sat up in coaches all the way and were snowbound for twenty-four hours between Albany and Buffalo. When the weary travelers finally arrived in Chicago, they were cold, hungry, and dusted with cinders.

Daisy liked her Northern grandparents very much. Grandfather and Grandmother Kinzie thought their grandchildren were beautiful even though they were very thin and pale and had boils and dull hair. Grandmother stuffed the girls with foods they didn't have back home.

The grownups laughed when little Daisy asked for "some of that nice little beefsteak with legs." She meant roast chicken, which she'd never seen before.

The Gordon girls had fun in Chicago, where they spent eight months. They saw their first snow there.

Grandfather John Harris Kinzie was still a government Indian agent. The Native Americans came to him with their problems, and they often stopped in Chicago to ask his advice before going to Washington to put their grievances before the president. It delighted Daisy to see the Native Americans sitting in silent conference with her grandfather in the garden.

During quiet times, Grandfather Kinzie told the children stories. Daisy's favorite was the true story about her great-grandmother, Eleanor Lytle McKillip, who, as a child, had been kidnapped and then adopted by the Seneca. Daisy knew that her great-grandmother had been named "Little-Ship-Under-Full-Sail" by Chief Cornplanter. Her mother had been called that name, too. So Daisy was proud when her family decided that it suited her. It was a good name for Daisy. Like a ship with sails spread and flags flying, she went through life proudly and fearlessly, in spite of strong winds and stormy seas.

In later years, Daisy told the story about her great-grandmother and the Seneca often—many times to Girl Scouts around a campfire. And throughout her life she smiled when people called her "Little-Ship."

Soon after the Gordons arrived in Chicago, Daisy became ill with a disease called "brain fever," perhaps as a result of years of poor nutrition and the exhausting journey from the South. For days no one knew if she would live or die. Finally the terrible fever broke, and she was out of danger. The doctor told the family that she was to have her own way until she was completely well.

Everyone brought Daisy gifts and fussed over her. She loved the attention. But several times when she was cranky, her grandmother told Daisy's mother she was afraid that Daisy would be spoiled for life. Her mother laughed and said that Daisy was the kind of person who would always have her own way.

On April 9, 1865, the family was about to have supper when they heard cowbells. Grandfather Kinzie burst in, shouting, "The war is over! The war is over!" They all ran out and joined the neighbors, who were ringing bells, hugging, laughing, and crying.

Daisy and Nelly jumped up and down, "We've won! We've won!" they cried. Grandpa Kinzie put his arms around the little girls and said, gently, "No, my dears, you've lost."

Daisy, in tears, ran to the gate on Michigan Street. Crowds of happy people were pushing past and shouting, "Hurrah for Lincoln and the Union!" and "Yea, General Grant!"

Men tossed their hats into the air and sang "Battle Hymn of the Republic," a favorite Yankee hymn. Daisy was not to be outdone. She quickly climbed the fence and loudly sang out "Dixie," a popular song of the Confederacy. The song, written by an Ohioan, had always been a favorite of Mr. Lincoln. So, for a moment, the Yankee crowd was quiet. Then they broke into cheers for the young Rebel.

It was difficult for Daisy to understand what had happened. Papa had lost! The Confederacy was gone. "Gone where?" she asked, bewildered.

Soon after the war's end, Grandfather Kinzie died. It was a sad time for the family. Daisy missed her grandfather who had told so many wonderful stories about the Native Americans and called her "Little-Ship-Under-Full-Sail."

In August 1865, Daisy and her family went back to Savannah to live with Grandmother Gordon. Mr. Gordon's cotton business had been ruined, but luckily there was some money to start over.

Grandmother Gordon's house needed a good cleaning. It was dusty and muddy from soldiers' boots. All that was left in the kitchen were two cups and a few saucers, some serving dishes, a teakettle, and an iron "spider" frying pan. But the house had escaped major vandalism. The only things stolen were the china, glassware, and kitchen utensils. Everyone was relieved.

The girls raced all through the house and out into the garden. Daisy would miss Grandmother Kinzie, but she was overjoyed to be home.

After the war, life in the South was difficult. The pastures had been turned into battlefields, and many of the farm animals killed. The cotton and other crops had been burned to the ground, and without slaves, there were few farmworkers. Food was still scarce. Taxes were high, and there was no money to pay them.

Yet Daisy and her sisters didn't think about money. They spent their days playing with their cousins, the Andersons, who lived nearby. They often met under a huge pittosporum tree that grew right in the middle of Grandmother Gordon's garden. Its heavy branches spread low and wide, making a cool, green playhouse.

Daisy loved animals, and she was always adopting starving, dirty cats and dogs. She faithfully fed and cared for her strays.

All her life, Daisy's heart went out to suffering animals. One freezing night, she pinned the best guest-room coverlet around a shivering cow. Imagine her mother's anger when, the next morning, she found the coverlet trampled on the stable floor!

When Daisy was fifteen, a calf died, and the mother cow went charging wildly about the yard, not letting anyone near her calf. Daisy put her arms around the unhappy mother's neck and wept with her.

Even when she was grown-up, Daisy loved animals and was full of sympathy for them. She always said an animal can be your best friend in life. One time in Atlanta, not wanting to spend two dollars for a taxi, she hired a horse-drawn cab for a dollar to take her to her hotel. The horse looked thin and sickly. When Daisy left the cab, she gave the driver a five-dollar bill and told him, "Now give that bag of bones of yours a good meal."

The first school that Daisy and Nelly attended was

at the home of Mlle. Lucille Blois on Chippewa Square, just a short walk from their house. Daisy learned to read from a book called *Little Tales for Very Little Children*. Every word in the book had three letters. Daisy liked to read about "Sam and his Dog." Mlle. Blois also taught Daisy manners, French, geography, history, spelling, and arithmetic.

Although Daisy did well in most of the subjects, she had a strange way of doing her addition and subtraction. And her spelling was awful. Daisy loved to draw, though. Often she was found drawing in her copybook instead of doing her arithmetic or spelling.

Daisy's brother Bill was born the year she started school. He was a lively redhead whose temper matched his red hair. Mrs. Gordon was pleased because she'd always wanted a son.

As Mr. Gordon built up his cotton trading business and became more prosperous, he rented other houses near Grandmother Gordon's, so there would be more room for his growing family. Still, the children played every day in Grandmother Gordon's garden, often with the Andersons, who now lived right next door. One year, the Gordon and Anderson cousins rigged up a "telephone" between the two houses. One small wheel was attached to a window at the Gordon house and another to a window at the Anderson house. On a string that ran between, a basket with messages was pulled from one house to the other. The message Daisy found most often in the basket was, "This very day at a quarter past three, we all will meet under the 'spittosporum tree'."

On winter evenings, the Andersons and Gordons often got together for a taffy pull. Cane syrup, flavorings, and a little vinegar were boiled on a huge coal-burning stove. When the syrup began to cool, the children pulled it so that it would not harden, but would stretch into soft, golden-brown taffy.

Daisy had long, light brown hair. One night at a taffy pull, her cousin Randolph Anderson suggested that they braid the sticky warm taffy into her hair to see if the two were really the same color. Daisy was willing. Soon the sticky candy was "braided" in her hair, and no matter how the children tugged and pulled, they couldn't get it out.

In those days it was not usual or appropriate for a girl to have short hair, unless she had been ill. Mrs. Gordon was very angry, and she, too, tried to remove the taffy. But it was stuck, and finally Daisy's mother had to cut off her daughter's lovely hair.

In September 1870, when Daisy was ten, something dreadful happened. Grandmother Kinzie and the Gordons were staying together at Amagansett, Long Island, in New York State. One afternoon, as Grandmother Kinzie sat on the lawn correcting proofs of her latest novel, she felt a cold coming on. She sent to the doctor for two-grain quinine pills to ward it off. The pills came in an unmarked box, and Grandmother Kinzie didn't want to take them. She wasn't sure they were the right ones.

"Nonsense," said Daisy's mother. "They must be

Mrs. Gordon cuts the taffy
out of Daisy's hair.

quinine since that was what you asked for." To show her mother that the pills were safe, Mrs. Gordon swallowed one herself. Grandmother Kinzie was convinced and took two. Not long after that, she became very ill. Another doctor was quickly called, but within four hours Grandmother Kinzie was dead! It was later found that the druggist had made a terrible error. Instead of quinine, he had sent pills containing morphine, which is poisonous if taken in large amounts.

Mrs. Gordon, who was expecting a baby, became terribly ill, too. But she hadn't taken as much morphine as her mother had. She was in so much pain she wanted to die, but Daisy's father fought hard to save her life. He forced her to walk, and he walked beside her—back and forth, back and forth—until at last the doctor said she would survive.

It was no wonder that in late October, when Nelly and Daisy came home from school and saw the doctor's buggy outside again, they were afraid to go in. It had only been a month since Grandmother Kinzie had died. Was someone ill again?

To their relief, the girls found that everything was fine. Mama was resting comfortably, and they had a new little sister, Mabel. Daisy's last sibling, George Arthur, whom they called Arthur, was born two years later, in August 1872. Now there were six Gordon children—four girls and two boys.

There was great love between Daisy's parents, and the Gordons were a warm, high-spirited, close-knit family, where individual differences were encouraged. William Gordon, Daisy's father, was an honest, loyal man with an excellent sense of humor. He was a good husband and father. Although Daisy loved both of her parents, she had a special relationship with her father.

Daisy's mother was very direct with her children. Once in a letter to Daisy, she commented on her daughter's bad spelling. "One more scolding before I finish up," she wrote. "I send a list of your words spelt wrong and the right way to spell them. Please study them hard, as you frequently, in fact always, spell them wrongly."

Daisy's Spelling	Right Way
sleave	sleeve
idear	idea
disgrase	disgrace
suspence	suspense

The Gordon children spent many summers at their Aunt Eliza Stiles's home at Etowah Cliffs, in northern Georgia. The huge house was on a cliff above the Etowah River. At times there were twenty cousins there. Etowah Cliffs was paradise for all the children. There were donkeys and goats to care for and lovely orchards and miles of forest to explore. They loved to climb trees, swim, and ride horses.

Sometimes the boys and girls split up. The girls made paper dolls and played hide-and-seek among the tangy-smelling pines. When they tired, they would lie on a bed of pine needles listening to the wind.

The boys mostly played Indians or "war," with Confederates against Yankees. They didn't let the girls join in their games very often. But once Daisy was "imprisoned" as a Yankee spy in the knothole of an oak tree. Eventually she was released, but after that the girls didn't play soldier games.

The children always loved theatricals. Daisy and the others at first improvised and later wrote plays and directed and acted in them. Daisy was considered the most talented actress. The dramas included stories from the Civil War, the life of Mary, Queen of Scots, adaptations from popular books, and the story of Little-Ship-Under-Full-Sail and the Seneca. The performances were given in the harness rooms and on the river cliffs, and they grew more and more elaborate.

The children also put out a magazine. It included many of Daisy's drawings. She also wrote many funny stories and poems. When she was eight or nine, she had written a poem called, "The Piggy." The first verse was,

> I was passing by a pig-stye,
> When I heard a piggy say,
> I would like to live in rubbish
> Forever and a day.

On hot days, everyone swam in the river, the swimmers often singing as they floated along. At night they sat around the campfire and watched the stars.

Chapter Two

Daisy Grows Up

Just before her fourteenth birthday, Daisy's parents decided to send her to boarding school with her sister Nelly. Daisy was growing up. It was time for her to say goodbye to her playhouse under the tree, her dolls, and her pets.

One crisp fall morning, dressed in new plaid dresses with matching bonnets, the sisters left for a school in Virginia called Stuart Hall. Daisy promised herself to do her best in school. She would try to behave and never quarrel with Nelly. Daisy really meant to be good, but it didn't always work out that way.

Life at school was hard. Daisy was used to climbing trees, riding horses, and running through the woods free as a butterfly. She missed her family. At home everyone liked her jokes and tricks. They laughed and called them "Daisy's stunts." But at school, the teachers didn't think she was funny. They were always telling her to keep still. She had to study hard to please her father. One time, in a letter to her mother, she begged to stop school. She wrote, "I hate it so and I can't believe I learn a thing."

Another time she wrote her mother, "If I get a low mark in French this month don't be surprised, because twice Miss B. has taken off my marks for drawing in class and it is hard work to pay attention in her stupid old class, but I will try."

Most of her letters, though, were full of news about school and her sister, explanations about money or requests for money, and little pictures.

Daisy did well in English and history. As for spelling, she was never to conquer it. When she was grown-up, Daisy told her brother, "Arthur, there is just no use in my having a dictionary. Here I want to know how to spell *scent*, you know, *scent* [of a flower.] And I've looked under *se* and *ce* and it isn't here at all."

Daisy still loved animals and birds. In another letter she told her mother, "We found a little robin frozen to death and we gave it a burial next day at recess. I got a little brown pasteboard box, just the shape of a coffin, and put pins in the edge of the lid, and they looked like silver-headed nails; and I made him a little shroud and a little cap, and laid him out on my doll's bed; and we had six pallbearers and I was parson and we had the services in the schoolroom."

One vacation, while Daisy was home from school, she saw some ragged children playing. They were Italian immigrants whose parents sold vegetables and fruits from a cart. She decided to organize a club to sew clothes for the poor. She called her club the "Helpful Hands."

Neither Daisy nor any of her friends knew how to sew very well, but did that bother Daisy? Not one bit. She named herself instructor of sewing, and went on to teach the others. At the first meeting, she made the other girls thread their needles with their left hands. From that time on, her brothers and sisters teasingly called Daisy's club the "Helpless Hands."

The girls worked hard and made some clothes to give to the poor children. But two of the boys got into a fight while wearing their new outfits. The clothes were not very sturdy and they quickly fell apart. So the boys had to run home, leaving their new clothes behind. Nevertheless, the girls had a good time with their club and continued to meet until the summer of 1876.

That year, when Daisy was fifteen, there was a yellow fever epidemic in Savannah. Several of the Italian children and one member of the sewing club died. Mr. and Mrs. Gordon wanted to send their children to Etowah Cliffs, but Nelly and Daisy, who had both been away at school all year, had earlier begged their parents to let them remain in Savannah. The Gordons agreed to let them stay home on condition they not leave the house after dark. Neither were they to go out in the heat of the day nor appear in the sun without a hat. And above all, they were never to open a window after sundown. People then believed that night air could cause yellow fever; nobody knew that mosquitoes carried the disease.

Daisy and Nelly spent many fun-filled summer

days renewing friendships with their Anderson cousins. Then in late August, one of Mrs. Gordon's dearest friends died of yellow fever. More cases were reported. Mr. Gordon told his wife to take the children to Etowah Cliffs until the first frost. It was believed the danger from the disease would be over then. Mrs. Gordon didn't want to go without her husband. But he wouldn't leave because he belonged to the Savannah Benevolent Association, an organization set up to help others in time of trouble. Mr. Gordon said his place was in Savannah.

"Then my place is right here with you," said Mrs. Gordon.

Finally Mr. Gordon came up with a compromise. His wife would take the children to Etowah Cliffs, leave them with Aunt Eliza, and she would stay in Guyton, only twenty miles from Savannah. He would come to Guyton by railroad every night. Daisy's mother had to give in.

The disease became a raging epidemic, and many people died. Mr. Gordon didn't go to Guyton, but his wife reluctantly forgave him because he was busy nursing the sick. She, too, spent most of her time nursing friends and relatives in Guyton who had contracted the disease. Fortunately, none of the Gordons got yellow fever.

It took until November for the epidemic to run its course, for the mosquito-killing frost was late that year. By that time, Daisy had returned to Stuart Hall. This time her sister Alice went with her, and Nelly was sent to Edge Hill, another Virginia boarding school.

The Christmas Daisy was sixteen, she and Alice

spent their holiday in Washington, D.C., with relatives. Although they had quarreled when they were younger, the sisters got along better as they went to their first grown-up parties and dances. Daisy was interested in boys, parties, and clothes. She also worried about her looks. In a letter to her mother she wrote, "My nose is getting 'trenormous,' much bigger than yours ever was! I am so disgusted!"

In due time, Daisy and Alice moved on to Edge Hill, while Nelly attended Mesdemoiselles Charbonniers, a French finishing school in New York City.

Once again, Daisy tried to get along with Alice, whom she still sometimes found "disagreeable." And she tried to follow the rules at Edge Hill, but there were just too many.

"Mama," Daisy wrote in a letter, "I can't keep all the rules. I'm too much like you. I'll keep clear of the big scrapes, but little ones I can't avoid."

Daisy got into trouble for eating food after lights were supposed to be out and for scaring the girls with ghost stories. She was given so many punishments that she told her sister, "Sometimes I think this place should be called Edge of Hell instead of Edge Hill."

Spelling was still a big problem for Daisy. She often got confused about the meanings of words, and her mistakes made the girls laugh. But she didn't mean to be funny, and she was indignant when others laughed at her.

Daisy had not conquered arithmetic, either. Her brother Arthur wrote later, "Two by two by no means made four to Daisy. They made anything she chose to imagine they made."

Although Daisy showed talent in art, she was not allowed to draw what she wanted because most of the time her teacher assigned drawing exercises. So sometimes she would slip away to the nearby woods to model clay or make pencil sketches of animals.

While at Edge Hill, Daisy pulled one of her so-called "Daisy stunts." She decided to follow a recipe she'd read in a girls' magazine for getting rid of the white flecks on her fingernails. She mixed the ingredients in a soap dish, then put her fingers into the solution. Within a few minutes, they were firmly cemented to the soap dish! She was very embarrassed when she had to be rescued by her teachers.

When Daisy graduated from Edge Hill, she received a silver medal for drawing. She would rather have had a scholastic medal to please her father. In Mr. Gordon's first letter to her at Edge Hill, he had told her to work hard on everything but drawing. Would her papa think she'd paid too much attention to art? She hoped not.

Daisy was relieved when her father said she'd done very well. Then her parents told her they were sending her to the Mesdemoiselles Charbonniers school in New York City, from which Nellie had just graduated. At that time, many girls were sent to finishing school to complete the training in academic and social skills that they needed to be "ladies." Perfect manners and fluency in several languages were required for graduation. Daisy's mother felt foreign language study was very important.

Daisy was thrilled to be going to New York City. Nelly had told her all about the exciting things to see and do there. She'd shop on Fifth Avenue and see plays and operas!

When she arrived in the fall of 1879, Daisy was almost nineteen. It was the first time she'd been at school without a sister. Nelly was home in Savannah, and Alice was still at Edge Hill. At first, Daisy was lonesome. As always, she missed her family when she was away from home. She wrote many letters to them, as she was to do all her life.

Her mother had accompanied her to school. When Mrs. Gordon left, Daisy wrote, "You don't know how I love you, my dear little mother! Neither did I, until you left me."

But it didn't take Daisy long to become adjusted and make friends. At "the Charbs," as the girls called the school, the classes were held in French. Students had to wear long black aprons over their dresses, and there were many strict rules. The girls were not allowed on the street alone. To exercise, they promenaded in pairs up Madison Avenue, always under the watchful eye of a teacher.

For the most part Daisy behaved very well. But one time she and some other girls got into a snowball fight, and they were kept in for three days as punishment.

Daisy studied hard and wrote letters home in French. Mabel and Arthur had a French governess and had learned French along with English. Arthur, who was then seven, wrote Daisy not to use French in her letters "because you can't spell in French either!"

Daisy, being older than her classmates, was allowed to make a special study of art. She did make progress. That spring, she painted from a live model. Painting made her heart sing. She told her friends that it was her greatest joy.

During Daisy's years at school, her family moved back into the Gordon house to live with aging Grandmother Gordon. Her front and back parlors, separated only by large pocket doors which slid into the walls, were perfect for dances and amateur performances.

When Daisy had finished a year at the Charbs, she was ready for her debut. A debut meant Daisy would be introduced to adult society in Savannah at her first formal ball.

Afraid of being a wallflower, Daisy had put off her debut as long as possible. But she needn't have worried. She was a great success as a debutante and became one of the most popular girls in Savannah. Witty, charming, and ready to try anything, Daisy liked being with people, and she was happy when others were having a good time.

In the fall of 1880, Daisy was looking forward to spending another year at the Charbs studying painting. Her parents wanted Alice to go on to the Charbs so Daisy was returning to keep her company. Alice had grown to be quiet and studious and was turning out to be the family beauty. She and Daisy had become the best of friends. Alice didn't want to leave Edge Hill, but her mother insisted, and Daisy kept telling her sister how much fun they would have together in New York City. So Alice finally agreed to go.

In early December, Alice became ill with scarlet fever. The Charbonnier sisters sent for Mrs. Gordon, and Daisy stayed with her sister until her mother came.

As she'd done when Daisy was near death, Mrs. Gordon sat day and night at her sick child's bedside. On December 10, Daisy wrote her father that Alice was much better and that the rash had left her face. But soon Alice took a turn for the worse. The doctors didn't know how to help her, and she died on December 30, 1880.

Dear, gentle Alice gone! Daisy and Nelly comforted each other as best they could. Mrs. Gordon, in terrible pain, blamed herself for making Alice go to New York. If she hadn't insisted, her daughter would never have gotten sick, she said over and over. And Mrs. Gordon, who ordinarily hated gloom, fell into deep mourning. The Gordon house, usually full of fun and laughter, was as quiet as spring without birds.

The family dressed in black, and everyone talked in hushed tones. It was with great sorrow in her heart that Daisy went back to school a few months later. Spring and summer went by, and still Mrs. Gordon grieved. When school was over, she kept her children cooped up in the house until her husband decided that it was unfair to them.

In September, he sent them off to visit friends and relatives. They were allowed to take off their mourning crepe—the bands of black material worn around their arms—but had to continue to dress in black. In October, Daisy wrote her mother, "You probably have not thought my grief profound because I throw it off. There is no need to analyze what I feel and it is when I am by myself that I feel it most. There is more than one kind of sorrow, and that borne in silence is not less genuine because it is not always seen."

Daisy's mother was grief-stricken for years, but the rest of the family managed to pull together their strength and courage and stop crying. Alice would always remain in their hearts and memories.

By the summer of 1882, Daisy was again busy with her social life. She was in demand for picnics, parties, boat races, and balls. She even received several offers of marriage. It was also that summer that Grandmother Gordon died. She was the last of Daisy's grandparents, and Daisy had been very fond of her. Daisy lovingly supported all her siblings, her Aunt Eliza, and especially her father in their grief.

Also that summer, Mr. Gordon gave Daisy her first trip to Europe. In England, Daisy visited the Low family at Beauchamp Hall. Andrew Low was a business acquaintance of her father. The Low girls were very friendly, and Daisy met their brother, Willie, whom she found charming. When Willie visited her in Savannah the following fall, Daisy told a friend that she had fallen madly in love with him. She didn't tell her parents, though, because she knew her father would not approve of Willie. He had been born rich, and he had never worked or supported himself. He depended on his father for everything. Mr. Gordon had always warned his daughters against marrying a man who didn't work for his living.

When Daisy returned from Europe, she shuttled back and forth between friends and relatives along the East Coast. There were rounds of parties and good times. She came home to Savannah briefly and then restlessly would begin traveling again. All her trips were made with an escort and her parents' approval.

In January 1884, Nelly married Wayne Parker. For the first time since Alice's death, Mrs. Gordon came out of her mourning to join the celebration. She seemed herself again.

Daisy was now a young woman of twenty-four, and she was deeply in love with William Mackay Low. Billow, as she had lovingly nicknamed him (to distinguish among all the Bills and Williams in her family), had a zest for living that matched Daisy's. He was a tall man with blue eyes and blond hair, and Daisy said he was "beautiful, like a Greek god." The young couple became secretly engaged.

Billow Low's father was English. He had come to Savannah and made a fortune in the cotton business. Probably intending to settle there, he became an American citizen and married Billow's mother, a Savannah girl. They had a lovely old home in the city. But when Billow was only seven his mother died, and he and his father returned to England to live.

Billow had been brought up by his older sisters,

who spoiled him. Because he didn't have to work, he became what we would now call an "international playboy." His main interests were horses, hunting, and parties. Nevertheless, Daisy was determined that Billow would be her husband. She became convinced that if she didn't marry him, she wouldn't marry at all.

About this time, Daisy went to the doctor with a painful earache. She insisted that he use silver nitrate to treat it. This was a new cure she'd heard about. The doctor protested that he didn't know how to use the silver nitrate properly, but he couldn't change Daisy's mind.

The silver nitrate made the earache worse. For months Daisy was in pain; then a large swelling developed behind her ear. Her mother was furious that the doctor had allowed himself to be persuaded and had hurt her daughter. Her father had to take her to Atlanta to see an ear specialist. Finally the pain and swelling went away, but Daisy was left partially deaf in that ear for life.

At last Daisy and Billow Low found the courage to announce their engagement to their parents. Daisy's parents were against the marriage because Billow had no money of his own and no trade or profession to earn an income. Daisy's father finally wrote Andrew Low to ask what settlement he would make as the Gordons were not financially able to support Daisy as a married woman. Mr. Low made a settlement that was acceptable, and the engagement was formalized.

Mr. Low arranged for his son to have a generous income, and he agreed to repair and furnish a house in

Savannah for the couple. Billow also got a share of his father's cotton business. Mr. Low died before the wedding, so Billow inherited even more.

Juliette "Daisy" Gordon was married to William "Billow" Low on December 21, 1886, at noon in her family parish, Christ Episcopal Church, in Savannah. Daisy chose the same date as that of her parents' wedding because she hoped to be as happily married as they were.

She was a lovely bride, slender in a white wedding gown that showed off her tiny waist. She wore the exquisite jewels Billow had given her. He was an expert at judging gems and had selected each diamond that was set in Daisy's beautiful crescent and star pin. With her dark eyes shining, she walked down the aisle carrying a bouquet of lilies of the valley, her sister Alice's favorite flower.

The bridesmaids' dresses were of white chiffon. (White was considered the only appropriate color for Willie's sisters, who were still in mourning for their father.) Each girl wore a white chiffon bonnet and the brooch that the bridegroom had given her. It was a daisy of diamonds, with the year "1886" on the flower's stem.

After a wedding breakfast at the Gordon home, the bride and groom dressed for traveling and dashed for their carriage in a shower of rice. Their honeymoon was to be spent on St. Catherine's Island, not far from Savannah. A home had been loaned to them by a friend of Daisy's father, and they were to have it all to themselves.

But the honeymoon was not what they had expected. A day or two after they arrived, Daisy's good ear began to hurt. Soon the pain was unbearable. Finally she had to return to Savannah and see a doctor. The doctor found that a grain of rice thrown at their wedding had lodged in that ear. He removed the rice from her badly inflamed ear but injured her eardrum. After the infection was healed, Daisy discovered that she was totally deaf in that ear. Now Daisy could hear only partially in one ear, the ear that had been damaged by the silver nitrate.

Daisy and Billow dash for their
carriage in a shower of rice.

Chapter Three

Juliette "Daisy" Low

During the first months of their marriage, Daisy and Billow lived in the Low house in Savannah. It was a large, square building, and together with its gardens in front and back and a carriage house, it filled one of the lots facing Lafayette Square. With her father's assistance, Daisy had the house modernized before her wedding. Her mother helped her decorate and furnish it.

She was a busy, happy bride. She loved to have company, and with her staff of servants and especially her great cook, Mosianna Milledge, she soon became famous for her dinner parties. But Daisy knew their stay in Savannah was only temporary. Because his father had died, Billow needed to oversee business and properties in England.

The first summer of their marriage, Billow told her they couldn't put off the move any longer. Daisy didn't want to live in England. She was afraid she wouldn't fit into the social life there. The wealthy Englishmen whom Billow knew had no work or responsibilities. They spent their time giving elegant parties at their big mansions, riding majestic horses, and going hunting.

But Little-Ship needn't have worried about fitting in. When they arrived in England, she sailed into the social life. Like her mother, Daisy was witty, a brilliant storyteller, and lovely to look at. She excelled in swimming and tennis, was a skilled horsewoman, and enjoyed hunting. These accomplishments made her very popular with Billow's set. And Daisy's outgoing nature allowed her to slip easily into the circle of social events. For Daisy, life in England was very different from life in America. Her friends were dukes, duchesses, earls, and lords, and even Edward, Prince of Wales, who as the oldest son of Queen Victoria was heir to the throne. She wrote home that she felt like a character in a novel.

At first the Lows rented two homes, one in England and one in Scotland. In 1889, Billow bought Wellesbourne House, in Warwickshire in central England. The estate had a large, ivy-covered stucco house. And to Daisy's delight, there were stables for horses and dog kennels. She could have many pets.

The stable and the house both required alterations to suit Billow. While the house was being renovated, the Lows made a trip to Egypt. After she returned, Daisy made her formal entrance into London society. Wearing a white satin dress with a train six yards long, white gloves, and three plumes in her hair, she was presented at Queen Victoria's court. It took hours to progress through the line to the queen, and Daisy grew tired. Her train was very heavy, and she didn't feel like carrying her huge bouquet of flowers. So she set the bouquet on the bustle of the lady in front of her, who unknowingly carried it through all the rooms.

When she had settled in her new house, Daisy got a gray parrot and named it Polly Poons. She had also brought a mockingbird from Savannah. The little bird would sit on her shoulder and try to take her pen away when she was writing. Anyone seeing Daisy with her pets for the first time probably thought she was odd. But people soon became used to seeing Daisy with small dogs at her heels, Polly Poons on her shoulder, and a little mockingbird fluttering around her head.

Because her husband disapproved, Daisy didn't serve on boards of organized charities or do official volunteer work. But she had her own ways of helping others. She gave time and money generously to individuals and animals. One time she heard of a woman in the village who was an outcast because she was thought to have leprosy. Bringing a basket of food, Daisy went to see the woman every week and often stayed and read to her. She also regularly visited the workhouse at Stratford-on-Avon which housed people who were poor and had nowhere else to go.

In England, Daisy's staff of servants included Mosianna Milledge, her cook from Savannah. She served delicious Southern food such as hickory-cured ham and candied sweet potatoes. Daisy's English friends had never tasted anything like these foods. Soon Daisy's dinner parties were as famous in England as they had been in America, and Southern foods became popular with high society.

Although she was happy in England, Daisy kept in close touch with home. She often invited someone from the family to join her for the London "season," which consisted of formal dinners, balls, and theater parties. Or they would be invited to stay in Scotland in the fall for fishing and shooting parties. Sometimes she would take a relative along on a trip to Paris. Daisy also liked to bring her British friends to America. No matter how long she lived in England and traveled abroad, at heart she was always an American.

When people told her she was the life of the party, Daisy would laugh and say she couldn't hear half of what was being said so she had to take things into her own hands. She told funny personal experiences and anecdotes about her deafness in such a way as to capture everyone's attention and admiration. She was well known for using her hearing impairment to her own advantage, and she never complained.

One of Daisy's favorite stories was about an incident that happened when she was in Scotland. She was walking alone and came to a stream. The bridge was out, and someone had thrown a log across. A peddler was standing on the bank, leaning on a cane.

Daisy asked the man to help her across the log, explaining that her deafness affected her sense of balance. He shook his head and began to say something, but she could hardly hear and didn't try to listen. While the man was still protesting, she grabbed his arm and told him she would tip him well.

"Now you walk across," she ordered. "I'll follow with my hand on your shoulder." The man shrugged and stopped arguing. He climbed on the log and started across. She closed her eyes and followed him. Slowly, very slowly, they went. The peddler tapped the log with his cane as they inched along. When they'd finally reached the other side, Daisy opened her eyes and took a good look at the man. He was blind! "Why on earth didn't you tell me?" she asked.

"I kept trying to, ma'am," the peddler said. "You wouldn't listen!"

The Lows had been married five years when Daisy injured herself while she was hunting. The doctor told her she could no longer ride or hunt. It hurt Daisy to give up the sports she loved, and she felt worse when Billow and their friends went riding and hunting and left her sitting home alone.

With Billow away, Daisy was lonely. She wrote to Mabel, "I can hardly face the loneliness of the coming winter now that I cannot ride anymore."

Daisy was an American, whose parents and grandparents had loving and supportive marriages. Billow was an Englishman, whose aristocratic background taught him to view marriage more as a formal contract between individuals.

What should she do while Billow was gone? Daisy

turned to the art she had loved in school. Carving a mantlepiece for the smoking room in her home kept her busy for a while. Then she made several oil paintings of hunting dogs.

Daisy's biggest accomplishment was a pair of iron gates for the main entrance to Wellesbourne. She had never worked with metals before, but that didn't stop her. She started in a class with several other ladies. They learned ironmongery from the village blacksmith.

Daisy found that she liked ironwork. After completing a small project, she hired the blacksmith to work with her on gates to Wellesbourne House. Like all blacksmiths, she made her own tools. The smith made the frames of the gates, and she made all the delicate designs. The project took an entire winter. Her arms became so muscular they wouldn't fit into her tight stylish gowns.

As time went on, Billow was gone more and more. He'd be off with his friends to Africa to hunt big game or to Albania to track wild goats in the mountains. He was almost never with Daisy. And what Daisy wanted most was her husband's companionship. Without it, she felt isolated and neglected. She had not been prepared for an English upper-class arrangement. She didn't complain to her family, but they sensed she was unhappy. Her sister Nelly visited with her children, and her brother Bill kept in close touch, too. He was a lawyer now and married, with a son. Mr. and Mrs. Gordon allowed Mabel and Arthur to spend a great deal of time with Daisy. Mabel came to England so often that she met and married an Englishman,

Rowland Leigh, and later settled there.

Daisy never lacked for dinner invitations. A favorite friend was Rudyard Kipling, the famous British author of *Just So Stories* (written in 1902). There was a brook filled with trout at the foot of the Kipling garden. One evening, after a formal dinner, Daisy decided to try her luck at fishing. Standing on the bank in her evening dress, she caught a big trout. Then Rudyard Kipling, dressed in dinner clothes, had to lie on his stomach taking Daisy's commands while he tried to net the catch. Laughing so hard they could barely breathe, the two fishermen finally captured the flopping fish.

The Spanish-American War began in 1898, and Daisy's father was made a brigadier general in the United States Army Volunteers. (He was one of the first Confederate officers to be made a general in the United States Army.) Cuba, an island near Florida, was then owned by Spain, and the Americans were fighting for Cuba's freedom. Daisy went to Miami, Florida, to help her mother set up a convalescent hospital for the men in General Gordon's brigade.

Daisy threw herself into hospital work with her usual energy and enthusiasm. It felt good to be needed. She used her wit and humor to keep the men happy, and she did the work of two people.

One evening, there was no milk in the hospital for the typhoid patients, so Daisy went out with an orderly to find some. There was none to be found in the entire town, but she remembered seeing some cows in a certain yard.

When she reached the house, the woman told her all the milk had been sold.

"What time were the cows milked last?" Daisy asked.

"At four o'clock."

"Then there should be enough milk to see our very sick men through the night."

"Maybe," said the woman, "but my hired man has gone home—he does the milking."

"I'll milk the cows," Daisy said.

The orderly held the lantern while Daisy milked. She'd learned to milk a bit at Etowah Cliffs when she was a girl, and with some perseverance she managed to remember how it was done. Soon there was a full pail to take to the hospital.

When the war was over, Daisy went back to England. As her brother Arthur grew older, Daisy began confiding in him. In 1899 she wrote Arthur that she seldom saw her husband and that the only love and affection she could count on was from her family. But Daisy remained devoted to her Billow, the charming, grown-up child who acted more like a bachelor than a responsible husband. Billow knew he could hurt Daisy because she loved him so much, and he often did hurt her with his excessive drinking and cruel jokes.

Early in 1901, Queen Victoria died, and Billow's friend, the Prince of Wales, became King Edward VII of England. By this time Daisy had to acknowledge, and her family could all see, that her marriage had failed.

Billow began to drink even more. His alcoholism was a sickness that he couldn't or wouldn't fight. He was often mean and moody. Daisy felt helpless as her husband's condition grew worse. In August, she told friends that Billow was away trying to cure his drinking and smoking habits. But what she didn't tell them was that he was staying with Mrs. Bateman, a beautiful widow whom he had been seeing for some time.

Billow became mentally and physically weaker. Although he continued to be fond of the Gordons and to provide money and gifts, he was increasingly cruel to Daisy, eventually even allowing Mrs. Bateman to act as mistress and hostess in their home. It was a sad time for Daisy, especially when Billow told her he wanted a divorce to marry Mrs. Bateman. Daisy didn't want a divorce; she still loved her husband. She told herself his brain had been affected by drinking, and that he was not responsible for his actions.

Daisy expressed her sorrow over her marriage in a poem she wrote and sent to Arthur in 1903:

> *The Road*
> The road which led from you to me
> is choked with thorns and overgrown.
> We walked together yesterday
> but now . . . I walk alone.

Billow tried to force Daisy to divorce him. The proceedings dragged on for years and would probably have gone on longer, but Billow died suddenly in 1905.

Upon his death Daisy said, "We all adored him and must feel that death was best for him, since his health and his brain were gone." Friends admired Daisy's quiet dignity at the time of her husband's death.

Billow left almost all of his enormous fortune to Mrs. Bateman. At the insistence of her father and brother, Daisy fought the will in court, along with Billow's sisters Mary and Jessie. Daisy won a flat sum and shares in the Low business. She also got the properties in America, including the house in Savannah, because of a technicality which made Billow's will invalid in Georgia.

At the age of forty-six, Daisy was a restless, lonely widow. She'd been married to Billow for nineteen years. She had no children though she seldom spoke of this sorrow. She felt there was no purpose to her life. She longed to do something worthwhile. She wrote of plans to become a sculptress, or to start some kind of work.

But she returned to her old life of parties and travel. Daisy was willing to go anywhere and do anything that promised activity. She had a home in Savannah and she bought another in London, and she rented a small house called Lochs in Scotland for the hunting season. Sometimes she rented her homes out to bring in income. She moved around so much it seemed as if she didn't live anywhere.

Her older nephews and nieces prized a trip with Aunt Daisy. She would take them to England or Scotland or even to India. The younger children in the family shared the trips in the fascinating stories she told when she returned.

Once she took a friend's two young daughters on a trip to Egypt. On the ship, Daisy decided to make a clay bust of the younger girl. She worked on it for two hours every morning of the long voyage. When they finally arrived in Egypt, Daisy impulsively tossed her work into the sea. She said it was no good.

The Low party climbed the pyramids, rode donkeys, shopped in bazaars, visited a harem, and drank gallons of strong Turkish coffee. Daisy dashed from one place to another, and the young girls had a hard time keeping up with her. She was interested in everything, and she never seemed to get tired. One of the girls summed up the trip: "It was romance. It was adventure. Through Daisy's eyes I saw. Through her mind I appreciated."

Even if Daisy was halfway around the world, she would return to Savannah for Christmas. Her nieces and nephews loved Aunt Daisy. They were delighted when she arrived laughing and full of fun, with a bird on her shoulder. She brought unique gifts from faraway lands for everyone. Although Daisy found it difficult to hear what was being said, she enchanted the children with her games and stories.

Daisy still enjoyed giving parties and balls. Sometimes, though, she would forget she had invited people. Mabel's son, Roland Leigh, wrote about the time Daisy asked friends to a party at her home. When he and the others arrived, they couldn't find their hostess.

Roland went up to his aunt's room, and there she was in bed, doing her accounting. She had sorted her bills into four envelopes labeled "This Year," "Next Year," "Sometime," and "Never." Daisy still hadn't learned how to handle money. Her father or Arthur had to straighten out her financial messes.

Daisy looked up from her work. Surprised to see her nephew, she asked Roland why he was there.

"Aunt Daisy, do you realize you're giving a dance downstairs?" he said.

"Why so I am," she replied. "I'll be down in five minutes."

"And she was," said her nephew.

Daisy bought a car in Savannah. There were no drivers' licenses or driving schools in those days. The dealer had only shown Daisy how to start and stop the car. When she wanted to go for a drive, she would tell her cook and butler to push the car out of the garage and turn it in the direction she was heading. While the fascinated neighbors watched, Daisy signaled the servants to stop traffic in both directions. Then she started the engine. With a great deal of sputtering, the car would leap forward or backward—Daisy never knew which—and off she'd go, hanging onto the steering wheel with one hand and waving gaily to her neighbors with the other.

Daisy was a very bad driver. One day, while rounding a corner, she lost control and smashed through the wall of a small wooden house. The car came to a stop in the dining room where a surprised family was eating. Without a word, Daisy backed out and called her brother Bill, who was a lawyer.

"What did you say to the people when you crashed into their house?" he asked.

"Why, I didn't say anything," she said. "I didn't think it would be polite to bother them while they were eating."

The years slipped by, and it was 1910. Daisy took a hard look at her life. She was now fifty years old. Her hearing was no better. She still thought of herself as a failure as a wife, and she brooded because she had no children. Worst of all, she felt nobody needed her. She was restless and unhappy.

Daisy again turned to her artwork. She went to Paris for sculpture lessons, then she came back to London. Again she was caught up in the whirl of luncheons, dinners, and balls. Then one day Daisy Low went to a luncheon that changed her life.

Chapter Four

Daisy's Girl Guides

It was May 1911, and the luncheon was like dozens of others Daisy had attended, with one exception. On this day she was seated next to a famous British war hero, Gen. Sir Robert Baden-Powell. He was the author of many books. And he was the founder of the Boy Scouts. Daisy had heard of him, but they had never met.

At fifty Daisy wasn't beautiful, but she was a striking woman with deep-set eyes and a straight, long nose. Although she couldn't hear much of what people said, they didn't notice because she was chatty and entertaining.

Though Daisy was in awe of Sir Robert, she held his attention when she told funny anecdotes about her sculpture classes in Paris. To her surprise, she found that the famous war hero, B.P., as she was to call him, was also an artist and sculptor. Moreover, he had been stationed in India, where Daisy had traveled.

Sir Robert was fifty-four years old, honorable,

dutiful, and unmarried when he met Daisy. He was a fine looking gentleman.

The luncheon led to a long friendship. Soon, their common interests led to their meeting again. Sir Robert took Daisy to meet Signor Lanteri, a teacher of sculpture whom he admired. Daisy was invited to join Signor Lanteri's class. She did join, and she enjoyed the lessons a great deal.

Sir Robert wrote many letters to Daisy. She always answered immediately. It was difficult for them to meet often because they were both so busy, but when they did get together, in London or Scotland, they found they had much to talk about.

Although Sir Robert was a soldier and a man of action, he gave Daisy a feeling of peace. She thought it was probably because he didn't seem to want anything for himself. He was always working for the good of others.

One evening when they were having dinner, Daisy told Sir Robert that she felt her life had been wasted. He patted her shoulder and said, "There are little stars that guide us on, although we do not realize it."

Daisy tried to find meaning in her friend's remark. She later wrote in her diary that her intuition told her B.P. believed she could make more out of her life. And perhaps if she followed his ideas, some useful work would open up for her.

That summer Daisy invited Sir Robert to Lochs, the house in the Scottish mountains that she rented for the hunting season. While he was there, B.P. and Daisy had time to talk about the Boy Scouts.

Sir Robert was interested in the many boys' groups that were springing up in England. He had given much thought to the education and training of young boys. He believed in teaching them to be physically fit, observant, honorable, responsible, and unselfish. Boys should not smoke or drink; they should do one good deed every day, and they should be encouraged to enjoy the outdoor life. In this way they would be happy and become good citizens.

Sir Robert put his ideas into a book called *Scouting for Boys*. It was published in 1908, and quickly became very popular. Almost every boy who read about Scouting wanted to join a patrol. Sir Robert left the military in 1909 and then spent all his time organizing the Scouting movement.

By the time Sir Robert met Daisy, there were forty thousand Boy Scouts in Great Britain, France, Germany, and the United States. And then Sir Robert told Daisy something that really caught her attention. Girls were just as excited about the idea of Scouting as boys. In fact, they had formed many troops on their own. Many girls had written Sir Robert begging him to start an organization for them but he had turned them down because he was so busy with Boy Scout work.

By the fall of 1909, six thousand girls were so eager to join the Boy Scouts that they had sneaked in by signing up using their initials instead of their names. Sir Robert's mother and sister, Agnes, persuaded him that proper young ladies could not be in the same movement as the boys. So busy or not, he had been forced to help form an organization for girls. That November he wrote the book *A Scheme for Girl Guides* in which he suggested ways to start patrols and train leaders. The Girl Guides would not be part of the Boy Scouts but a separate organization. The girls' uniforms would be blue instead of khaki.

Sir Robert asked Agnes to take charge of the Guides. In those days parents would have objected if their daughters ran around dressed in knickers like boys, with Scout knives dangling from their belts. Agnes Baden-Powell was a well-respected woman with excellent manners. People knew that nothing she was involved in would be unladylike.

Girls were very enthusiastic about their new organization. And the idea of the Girl Guides excited Daisy. She later wrote her father, "I like girls and I like the organization and the rules and pastimes, so if you find that I get very deeply interested you must not be surprised."

Daisy thought of the girls from poor families who lived on the farms of Glen Lyon near Lochs. They worked hard at house and farm work, but because of the long distances between the cottages they had practically no social life. When the girls were very young, they left the Perthshire Valley to work in factories and kitchens. Daisy told Sir Robert she was thinking of starting a Girl Guide troop in Glen Lyon.

Sir Robert understood Daisy. He knew she wanted

Album

Daisy, about ten years old.

Daisy and Billow's wedding party.

At left is a portrait of Daisy when she was about seventeen,
painted by Edward Hughes.

Daisy and some of her friends, about 1895, on a Scottish moor.
Daisy is the third person from the left.

Scottish Girl Guides.

Daisy at her desk at National Headquarters
in Washington, D.C.

Sir Robert Baden-Powell, Lady Baden-Powell,
and Daisy. This photo was taken in 1919,
when the Baden-Powells visited the United States.

Mrs. Calvin Coolidge becomes honorary president
of the Girl Scouts of the U.S.A. in 1924.
Calvin Coolidge was president from 1923 to 1929.

Daisy with some of her girls, in the backyard
of the Low house in Savannah.

Daisy with some American girls at Foxlease,
in England, at the Third World Encampment in 1924.

Daisy and Lady Baden-Powell at the
World Encampment at Camp Edith Macy,
Pleasantville, New York,
May 1926.

to devote herself to something worthwhile. He told her to take her time and think through her plans before she went ahead.

But as usual, Daisy threw herself into the project immediately, and with her whole heart. In August 1911, just three months after her first meeting with B.P., armed with the English handbook *How Girls Can Help to Build Up the Empire*, written by Sir Robert Baden-Powell and Agnes Baden-Powell, she invited every girl in Glen Lyon to her home for the first meeting.

Seven girls came, with one young woman walking seven miles. The girls were shy at first. They had seen Lochs castle all their lives, but they had never expected to be invited there. In her own charming way, Daisy told the girls about the Girl Guides, and it wasn't long before they were all talking together like old friends. The housekeeper served fresh strawberries and tea with delicious hot buttered scones, a small biscuitlike pastry. Afterwards, Daisy invited the girls to meet at her home every Saturday afternoon.

When they left, Daisy worried that the girls wouldn't want to come to another meeting because they had to walk so far.

But they did! And it wasn't just for the good food she served. They learned the Girl Guide promise:

> I promise on my honor that I will do my best
> To do my duty to God and the King
> To help other people at all times
> To obey the Guide law.

They also learned the Girl Guide laws and a history of the British flag. After the first few meetings, Daisy knew that the girls were having fun and that they enjoyed learning new things. She taught them how to administer first aid, tie knots, and read maps. Her patrol learned to cook good plain food they could afford. And Daisy taught them gardening, drawing, sewing, and even personal hygiene.

The meetings were always interesting. Some of Daisy's houseguests were soldiers who taught her patrol to march and drill and send messages with signals. When Daisy confided to Sir Neville Smyth, an officer who was staying with her, that she didn't know how to talk to the girls about the importance of using a toothbrush, the kindly general offered to do it for her. While giving the Guides a lesson on camping, he asked, "What is the very first thing you must take to camp?" The girls called out various things, and he replied, "Wrong answers! The first thing to take is your toothbrush!"

Daisy wanted her girls, who were from poor families, to be able to earn some money so they would not have to go away from home and work in factories. It occurred to her that they could raise and sell chickens and eggs to the hunters who stayed in the lodges during the shooting season.

The girls learned how to raise poultry, and the visitors bought eggs and chickens, but the season was too short for the patrol to earn much money.

Daisy thought of another fund-raising project.

At tea in Lochs castle, Scotland, Daisy tells local girls about the Girl Guides.

Sheep thrived in the valley. If the girls could spin the wool into yarn—good high-grade yarn—it should bring in money. Daisy would teach them to spin.

But first she had to learn how to spin herself. Why not? She was good at arts and crafts, and she had made her own ironworking tools, hadn't she? Daisy bought a spinning wheel and found a teacher. It didn't take her long to master the skill. Then the girls learned it.

When fall came and Daisy prepared to return to London, every Guide in her patrol had a nice flock of chickens. And the girls were so good at spinning that they could make yarn in the dark! Before Daisy left Lochs, she persuaded the village postmistress to take charge of the spinning project.

In London, Daisy found a little shop that made and sold handwoven articles. The owner agreed to buy all the yarn the Glen Lyon girls could make.

Throughout the summer, Daisy had been busy and happy. Helping a group of girls that needed her had made her feel useful. She told Girl Guide headquarters in London that she was going to start a Girl Guide patrol in the city, too.

Daisy rented a basement room large enough for patrol meetings and invited several neighborhood girls between the ages of seven and eighteen to come to a meeting. The few who came were timid. But at each meeting more girls joined them. Daisy's city patrol learned skills similar to those the Glen Lyon Guides had learned, but Daisy adapted them to city living. And as time went on the London group enjoyed being Girl Guides as much as the girls in Scotland did.

One day Daisy went through Lambeth, a poor section of London. She decided to start her second London patrol there. And as the weeks went by both groups thrived.

Everything was going so well that on December 14, 1911, Daisy gave a tea for sixty people, which included all the committees of Girl Guides in London. The organization was growing fast. Now it was time to get ready to leave for America.

Before leaving, she put her London patrols into the hands of able leaders. Daisy had a talent for making big plans and getting good people to carry them out. Daisy chose Mrs. Mark Kerr to take charge of her Lambeth patrol, even though she barely knew her. Using a hearing device with earphones, Daisy told Mrs. Kerr she was to direct the group. Mrs. Kerr refused. She told Daisy she had no time, didn't live in London, and was no good with girls.

"Then it's all settled," Daisy said cheerfully, tuning out Mrs. Kerr's protestations. "I have already told my girls you will take the meeting next Thursday." She left money for the Guides' uniforms and other expenses, told the astonished woman to be sure to "give them a good tea," and said that she would be back in six months.

Daisy wrote a fond farewell to her Scottish patrol, and on January 6, 1912, three months after she had started the first London patrol, she sailed for the United States. Sir

Robert was on the same ship. He was on his way to visit Boy Scouts around the world. Daisy was thinking about bringing Girl Guides to the United States. The more she thought about it, the more she liked the idea. She discussed her plans with B.P., and he was enthusiastic. Daisy spent hours asking his advice and taking notes.

On the ship Olave Soames, a pretty young woman, often joined B.P. as he sat on the deck. Later, Olave and B.P. became engaged.

As for Daisy, the one thing uppermost in her mind was to start Girl Guiding in America. And the place she planned to start was in her home city, Savannah. She was no longer a young woman, and the job ahead would be a difficult one. It would take all her strength and energy. She was deaf and frail. Yet when Daisy wanted to do something, nobody could stop her. And nobody was going to stop her now.

Chapter Five

Daisy and the Girl Scouts

As soon as Daisy arrived in Savannah, she phoned Nina Anderson Pape, a friend and distant cousin who was the headmistress of a girls' school.

"Come right over," Daisy said. "I've got something for the girls of America and all the world, and we're going to start it tonight!"

Nina had always liked Daisy, and she wondered what her cousin's latest wild idea would be. When Daisy told her about the Girl Guides, Nina was impressed. She agreed with Daisy that girls as well as boys should be taught to develop good qualities such as honor, kindness, loyalty, and thrift. Daisy's idea to train girls in both mind and body was something new, and it wasn't wild at all. In fact, Nina knew a group of girls in Savannah that could easily become Daisy's Girl Guide patrol. The girls met on Saturday afternoons with Walter Hoxie, a retired navy man who was a naturalist. During hikes in the woods, Mr. Hoxie taught them about trees, birds, and wildlife. Often the girls cooked supper over a campfire.

A made-to-order patrol! Daisy was delighted to find out that Page Anderson, her cousin Randolph's daughter, was one of the group. Daisy smiled to herself as she recalled the time when they were children and Randolph had braided taffy into her hair.

Soon afterwards, Daisy had dinner at the Andersons. As usual she was late, and they had started to eat without her. She came into the dining room tying knots in a strip of soft leather. Of course the Andersons wanted to know what she was doing.

"I'm learning to tie knots for my Girl Guides," she said.

The Andersons were very curious about the Girl Guides. So Daisy told them all about the organization and how English girls were begging to join. Page was so excited she demanded to know why American girls couldn't join, too.

Daisy replied that if Page and her friends wanted, she would help them organize a patrol and become Girl Guides.

Page was certain her group would accept Cousin Daisy's offer. She was right. The entire naturalist club came to the Gordon home to hear about Girl Guides and find out how to form a patrol.

The Sunday after the meeting, Daisy stopped Page Anderson's mother at church and told her that she had been appointed captain of her daughter's patrol. Then Daisy darted away without giving the startled Mrs. Anderson a chance to say a word.

On March 12, 1912, the day Page turned twelve years old, she and seventeen other girls twelve or older became the first officially registered Girl Guides in the United States. Two Girl Guide patrols were formed. The patrols were called the "Pink Carnation" and the "White Rose." Each girl had with her a notebook, a pencil, and a yard of cord to practice knot tying. Some younger girls were at that first meeting, but they could not register until they turned twelve. Over the next months, other patrols were officially registered.

It was a solemn occasion. The girls learned the Promise, which Daisy had changed for the American girls.

> On my honor I will try:
> To do my duty to God and my country,
> to help other people at all times,
> to obey the Girl Guide Law.

Then they signed their names. Daisy wrote the first name herself, that of her brother Bill's daughter, her twelve-year-old namesake, Margaret "Daisy Doots" Gordon. Bill and his family were living on a plantation twenty-three miles from Savannah. Doots had never even heard of the Girl Guides, and she had no idea her aunt was signing her up.

Patrol meetings were first held in a downstairs room of the Louisa Porter Home, a ladies' residence across from where Daisy lived. Later, the girls moved to the carriage house behind Daisy's home. A sign over the door said, "Girl Guide Headquarters." Outdoor games were played on a nearby vacant lot owned by Daisy. Enormous canvas curtains were strung on wires around the new basketball court to keep passersby from gaping. In those days, people didn't often see young ladies dressed in gym suits playing games on main thoroughfares, and they were curious. But the girls didn't care what others thought. Daisy was opening a whole new world to them. And Savannahians knew that anything a lady like Daisy Gordon Low was involved in must be proper.

The Girl Guides enjoyed everything about their new organization. They especially liked their uniforms. They had wanted to make them like the ones in the English Guides' handbook. After hours of cutting and recutting, pinning, and sewing, they succeeded. They were proud that their uniforms looked just like those worn by English girls.

For their middy blouses and long skirts, they chose a dark blue duck fabric. The garments had light blue trim. The girls made light blue sateen ties for their blouses, and completed their uniforms with black cotton stockings and big black hair ribbons. When they wore their uniforms around town, they caused quite a stir. Other young girls wanted to know how they, too, could become Guides.

Daisy went to all the patrol meetings. Each meeting began with the girls reciting the Promise and the Laws. Using the English handbook *How Girls Can Help to Build Up the Empire*, written by B.P. and his sister, the members worked to pass certain requirements for which they were given badges. To earn the Tenderfoot Badge (which was a brooch), a girl had to learn how to tie four knots, know the name of the governor of her state and the mayor of her city, and learn the history of the United States flag and how to fly it.

To earn a Second Class badge, a girl had to have been a Tenderfoot for a month and pass several tests such as cooking a potato or a small amount of meat, making a bed properly, and demonstrating what to do in case of fire. After earning a Second Class Badge, a girl could go on to more difficult tests and earn a First Class Badge. Most of the badges had to be hand-embroidered.

The Girl Guides also played games, went on hikes, kept bird notebooks, and formed a basketball league. The patrols enjoyed formal teas at Daisy's house.

Daisy's patrols were doing well. So putting her friends in charge, she took off for her brother Bill's house to tell her niece, Daisy Doots, she had been made a Girl Guide.

"You've made me a what?" Doots asked.

"A Girl Guide. All the girls of Savannah are going to be Guides."

Doots asked why, and Daisy told her because it was a wonderful thing to be. Then she casually added that she'd signed her niece up as the first member.

Doots was indignant. Daisy had no right to sign her up without her permission.

Daisy explained that she thought Doots would want the chance to learn how to cook and give first aid and tie knots. Then she slyly added that Doots would feel pretty silly when she saw that all the girls around Savannah were in uniforms covered with badges.

As soon as Doots heard about the uniforms and badges, her attitude changed. She became very interested.

Without wasting a moment, Daisy pulled out her strip of leather and began showing Doots how to tie a square knot.

So Daisy Doots became known as America's first official Girl Guide.

When Daisy returned to Savannah, she found that in the short time she'd been gone, four more patrols had been formed. There were now six, with memberships ranging from six to sixty. Daisy established a camp, Lowlands, for the girls to use as their very own.

Page's patrol had a five-night campout. The girls slept on the ground and got red clay all over their blue uniforms. They enjoyed cooking over an open fire, but they didn't like the mosquitoes—and there were plenty!

One of the leaders laughingly told Daisy about a first-aid lesson she'd given her patrol. After their instruction, the girls decided to buy adhesive tape and gauze and practice bandaging one another. Still wearing the bandages, they went to the home of one of the girls where their mothers were having a card party. The mothers saw their daughters with their heads and legs bandaged and their arms in slings, and several of them fainted.

When Daisy heard about the incident, all she said was that the girls must have done a professional job of bandaging!

Daisy was busy and happy with the Girl Guides. She wrote her sister Mabel, "You mustn't be bored with Girl Guides, as I can't think of anything else."

In May, she was off to England. She had great things to report to Sir Robert. They had dinner together when he returned to London from a world tour. Then Daisy spent her time catching up on Girl Guide activities in England.

While she was there, Mr. Gordon gave permission for Daisy's picture to appear in the local Savannah newspaper. Southern ladies did not usually allow their photos in newspapers and ordinarily such publicity wouldn't have been permitted, but Daisy's parents were doing everything they could to help Daisy with Girl Guides. They were not very impressed with the organization, and secretly, they thought their daughter would soon tire of this project as she had tired of so many others. But they were delighted that their Daisy, who had been through so much, was keeping interested and happy.

In September 1912, after a short illness, Daisy's father died. She was grief-stricken. How she had depended on her father's love! Over the years, they had kept in close contact through their letters. Daisy wrote her brother Arthur that her father hadn't loved her more than his other children, but because he knew she needed him more, he had tried to make up for all she lacked.

Yet Daisy could not give in to her sorrow. Her mother needed her. Mrs. Gordon was stunned and physically exhausted by General Gordon's death. Daisy took her to England to recuperate. After a while, Daisy was able to get away by herself and deal with her own pain. When she had her emotions under control, she put even more effort into her Girl Guides.

That fall Sir Robert and Olave Soames were married. Daisy visited the Baden-Powells at their home in England, and she and Sir Robert maintained their friendship throughout her life. As Olave became deeply involved in the Girl Guides, she and Daisy worked together for the movement. Daisy and the Baden-Powells visited back and forth, and she was happy for them when each child was born.

As for Daisy, the Girl Guides were the only children she would ever have. The organization took over her thoughts, her energy, her whole life. Daisy paid all the organization's expenses for the first four years, including those of her Girl Guide patrols in England and Scotland. Whenever she spoke of her work, she told people she didn't need their money, just their support.

There was much to do as more and more patrols were formed. New leaders needed guidance. A handbook for American girls must be written. Although the fundamental principles of the organization would be the same for the American girls, Daisy knew there were important differences between England and the United States. Great Britain was an empire with subjects in many lands. That's why B.P. and his sister had titled their handbook, *How Girls Can Help to Build Up the Empire*. But the United States was a democracy, with a different system of government and different laws.

In the spring of 1913, the first handbook for American girls, *How Girls Can Help Their Country, A Handbook for Girl Scouts,* was finished. Walter Hoxie, the naturalist, was the author, though Daisy had made suggestions based on the British handbook. In several places in the handbook, it seems as if she is speaking. This advice sounds like it comes from Daisy: "Boiling water is useful to dip your sardine into if you want to get his skin off, but do not dip him into the teakettle." Girls were told how to secure a burglar with eight inches of cord. "Make a slip-knot at each end of your cord. Tie the burglar's hands behind him by passing each loop over his little fingers. Place him face downwards, and bend his knees. Pass both feet under the string, and he will be unable to get away."

Girls were also advised that "'Keep your mouth shut,' is a good motto, not only so as not to breathe in dust and the seeds of disease, but also so as not to say things hastily that you will have to repent later. An employer once said that he never engaged a lad who carried his mouth open (boys who breathe through the mouth are generally stupid)."

Some of the advice in the 1913 handbook seems very modern, for example, the page on oatmeal. "Oats, too, are full of value; a pound and a half a day will keep a hard-working man, for oatmeal increases the power of the muscles, and is rich in bone and flesh-forming materials." The handbook also said, "Sun and air are life-giving," and "Drugs are bad things." It advised, "When mean girls want you to play in some low fun, when you think it is not right, ask yourself if mother would like to see you doing it; be brave, and have courage to say it isn't right."

In the early 1900s, many women were fighting for the right to vote. (It was not until 1920 that the Nineteenth Amendment was ratified, ensuring that no one can be denied the right to vote because of sex.) Daisy didn't fight for women's rights. She had been raised to be a cultured woman, to raise a family and run a home. But she believed that women should be active and independent, like her own mother and her pioneer ancestors.

Besides giving information on subjects such as first aid, homemaking, and outdoor living, the handbook encouraged girls to have careers. They were told they could be anything they wanted to be, that there were no occupations belonging solely to men. And examples were given of successful women in the fields of medicine, astronomy, chemistry—even women who had flown airplanes! "The numbers of women who have taken up aviation prove that women's nerves are good enough for flying," the handbook said. "Madame Dutrieu has made some splendid flights across country over hills and rivers, and lately she took a passenger with her in her biplane."

Some of the Savannah parents thought Daisy was teaching unladylike things. Their daughters were brought up to be ladies. And ladies should do nothing more strenuous than roll a hoop. Playing basketball or having a career was considered unfeminine.

Parents who allowed their daughters to join Girl Scouts admitted Daisy was odd in some ways, but they didn't believe she would teach unladylike things. She was after all, a Gordon—and a lady.

By the time the handbook was published, the name of the organization had been changed from Girl Guides to "Girl Scouts." In 1913, the Girl Scout law was:

1. A Girl Scout's Honor is to be trusted.
2. A Girl Scout is loyal.
3. A Girl Scout's duty is to be useful and to help others.
4. A Girl Scout is a friend to all and a sister to every other Girl Scout, no matter to what social class she may belong.
5. A Girl Scout is courteous.
6. A Girl Scout keeps herself pure in thought, word, and deed.
7. A Girl Scout is a friend to animals.
8. A Girl Scout obeys orders.
9. A Girl Scout is cheerful.
10. A Girl Scout is thrifty.

When the handbook was published, letters asking for information about Girl Scouts poured in from all over the United States. Daisy had been getting ready for this; she had started organizing in the Northeast in the summer of 1912.

Although she was still involved with her Savannah Girl Scouts, in June 1913 Daisy set up a national headquarters in the Munsey Building in Washington, D.C. She decided that an acquaintance, Edith D. Johnston, was to be the national secretary. Turning her deaf ear to Edith's protests, she took her on a visit to Washington, and while there, told her that she was to be in charge of national headquarters. Daisy bought furniture and hired a part-time office worker who was to take charge until Edith could be there permanently. The young woman was to open the mail, send all requests for information to Edith, and fill orders for the handbook.

Daisy traveled widely to organize new areas and to incorporate established troops into one national organization. She was the founder of the Girl Scouts of the U.S.A. and organizer of the American movement. Several other girl groups joined her Girl Scouts, but not Campfire Girls, which had been started in 1910. Robert Baden-Powell and the leaders of the American Boy Scouts hoped there would be only one American girls' movement, but for various reasons Campfire Girls and the Girl Scouts of the U.S.A. never merged.

Daisy asked all of her family and friends to help with Girl Scouting. Friends introduced Daisy to many influential people. One friend took Daisy to a reception at the White House. Nelly helped Daisy, too. She got Theodore Roosevelt's sister Corinne Robinson and Mrs. Thomas A. Edison interested in the movement.

Daisy even called on Mrs. Woodrow Wilson, the president's wife, to ask her to be honorary president of the Girl Scouts. Mrs. Wilson accepted. The First Lady is the honorary president of the Girl Scouts to this day.

Although Daisy had achieved much success, there

were still parents who doubted the value of Scouting and wrote critical letters to the local newspapers. "Girl Scouts and Boy Scouts roam the countryside together on what I can only describe as glorified larking expeditions. . . . Scouting for girls leads nowhere," one irate parent wrote. Another said, "We don't need an army of women—Morse signalling is not feminine and scouting leads to a decay of household arts."

In spite of the prejudiced few, Juliette Gordon Low was fast becoming a national celebrity. She still attended many dinners and luncheons, but now she was the main speaker. More and more reporters interviewed her for newspapers, and Mrs. Gordon was happy to see the success of her impulsive daughter. How proud she was when people called Daisy a genius!

Daisy still traveled restlessly, and she led a hectic social life. She never stayed anywhere long. She traveled back and forth between England, Scotland, and America. In England, she was presented in court to King George V and Queen Mary. And once while she was there, she managed to go for a ride in a monoplane.

But no matter where she was, Daisy kept in touch with her troops in Savannah by mail. She also wrote dozens of letters to the women who worked with her in Scouting about the design and production of badges, the distribution of the new handbook, her thoughts on selecting and teaching new leaders, and many other things pertaining to her beloved movement.

In September 1913, Edith Johnston at the

Washington Girl Scout headquarters received a cablegram from Daisy advising Edith to soon be ready to meet her in "New York, Baltimore, Washington, or Boston." They eventually got together in New York for a meeting where it was decided to have the Girl Scout uniforms manufactured. The organization was growing so rapidly that it was no longer practical or necessary for the girls to make their own.

Daisy took charge and found a manufacturer who used good materials and gave the best prices. The color khaki was first added as a practical alternative, then the color was officially changed to khaki. Blue showed dirt easily, was less popular in the years leading to World War I, and became expensive as indigo, the dye used for the blue cloth, was difficult to get during the war years. The Boy Scout officials complained, but they soon got used to seeing the girls in their colors.

Daisy was in Scotland on August 4, 1914, when Great Britain entered World War I. In December, she went back to London. She and Mabel worked to help war refugees who were fleeing to England.

Despite a heavy load of war work, Daisy kept writing to her Girl Scouts in America. She told them in great detail about the English Girl Guides' war activities. She also revised the Girl Scout handbook. Letters came back from America telling Daisy about all the new Girl Scout troops being organized. And because of Daisy's letters, American girls began raising money for war relief. It was the first of many international projects through which the American Scouts made friends all over the world.

In January 1915, Daisy heard that all five thousand copies of the 1913 Girl Scout handbook had been distributed. She headed for Savannah to get her revised edition into print. Friends were worried about her crossing the sea during wartime. They warned that the Atlantic was full of German submarines.

Submarines were only one of Daisy's problems. Her biggest concern was money. The cost of financing Girl Scouts was increasing with every new troop, and Daisy's income had been steadily decreasing. Where could she get money to pay for printing the handbook and producing uniforms and badges? When it was suggested that each Scout be asked to pay dues of twenty-five cents a year, she wouldn't hear of it. Daisy felt she must be responsible for the Girl Scouts and provide the money. So she decided to sell her pearls. Daisy knew the money from this sale wouldn't last long, but she said, "It will make it possible to finance the organization for some little time at least."

One of Daisy's fund-raising stunts was to trim her hat with a bunch of parsley and several carrots before going to a fashionable luncheon. When the vegetables began to wilt, she would say, "Oh, is my trimming sad? I can't afford to have this hat done over. I have to save my money for my Girl Scouts. You know about the Girl Scouts, don't you?" It was her way of calling attention to her pet project.

When the party was over, she would go up to one

of the guests and say, "I am so glad you are interested. You're exactly the type of person we need on that committee." Then turning her deaf ear to the refusal, she'd continue, "That's marvelous! I shall expect you at the committee meeting on Wednesday."

On June 10, 1915, the first Girl Scout Convention was held in Washington, D.C. A National Council was formed with Juliette Low as president. A constitution and by-laws were adopted, and the organization was incorporated under the laws of the District of Columbia.

Daisy continued to cross the Atlantic whenever she felt it was necessary. Not even the sinking of the British ship the *Lusitania* by the Germans in May 1915 frightened her.

Before leaving for England that summer, Daisy called on her goddaughter Anne Hyde Choate, the daughter of her best friend from their days at the Charbs. There was a new troop in Pleasantville, New York, where Anne lived, and Daisy wanted her to get involved. She told Anne it would just mean pinning on a few badges. Anne soon found out there was a lot more to it than that. But she stayed with Girl Scouting and eventually became president of the national organization after Daisy stepped down.

When Daisy arrived in England, besides doing her Girl Guide and Girl Scout work, she pitched in again and helped Mabel collect food and clothes for Belgian victims of the war.

Early in 1916, Daisy was back in America again.

Daisy wears vegetables on her hat to raise money for the Girl Scouts.

She moved the National Girl Scout headquarters from Washington, D.C., to New York. Daisy now had seven thousand Girl Scouts registered, and her schedule was busier than ever. From New York, she hurried to Philadelphia to make a speech for Girl Scouts. Then she went to Washington for a big Girl Scout rally attended by members of the Cabinet and other important people. After arranging for a big ball to be given by the Girl Scouts in Washington on March 4, she went off to Richmond, Virginia, to attend another Girl Scout meeting.

Meetings with Daisy were never dull. One day, a committee was to choose an official Girl Scout shoe. A sample pair had been purchased, but when it came time to talk about the shoes, nobody could find them.

"Where are the shoes?" someone asked.

"I've been wearing them all day," said Daisy. Without another word, she tucked her skirt between her knees and stood on her head to show them off.

On February 22, 1917, Eleanor Kinzie Gordon died. Daisy mourned her mother, who had always been a good friend and supporter. About two months later, Daisy stood looking out the window watching soldiers march by. Her heart was heavy for her mother and for the men who were on their way to fight overseas. On April 6, the United States had entered the World War.

The Girl Scout Board sent a telegraph to President Wilson volunteering to help in the war effort. Immediately, the Girl Scouts were put to work. To earn badges, they had always had to learn skills well enough to teach them and to be of service to others. Now they put their knitting skills to good use by making scarves and sweaters for the soldiers. They cleaned offices, got bandages ready for army hospitals, and ran messages for the Red Cross. They worked in canteens which were opened at railroad stations, sometimes making five hundred sandwiches a day for soldiers. They sold millions of Liberty Bonds, which helped to finance the war. Overworked nurses depended on them to help with patients during the flu epidemic that began in 1918.

When people realized how much help these trained groups of girls were giving to their country, more new troops of Girl Scouts sprang up. Now Daisy realized she didn't have enough money to keep all the troops going. She finally agreed to a fund-raising campaign. The committee members contributed $350 to start. Then they wrote letters asking people to be honorary Girl Scouts and give five dollars a year.

The campaign was successful. Daisy had accomplished wonders in a short time. In fact, the movement had grown so large there was a need for standards and supervision. But Daisy knew that given time, she would solve these problems. Her Girl Scouts were thriving.

Chapter Six

Daisy's Greatest Triumph

When the third National Girl Scout Convention was held in New York City, on October 26, 1917, there were more than fifty delegates present. They were leaders from all over the country. Daisy proudly reported that as a result of the publicity about their war work, Girl Scout troops had been organized in the territory of Hawaii and every state except Utah. She showed the first issue of the Girl Scout magazine, called *The Rally*. There were now 12,812 members. In less than six years, the Girl Scouts had grown from two groups of Savannah girls to a large national organization.

Daisy answered questions about the new Brownie program that had begun the previous year in Massachusetts. It had been started because younger girls wanted to belong to Girl Scouts, too.

The new handbook for Girl Scouts had been published, and it was selling as quickly as it rolled off the press. Daisy was so busy traveling around the country making speeches that she practically lived in her Girl

Scout uniform. Like the girls' uniform, the adult uniform was khaki-colored, but it was cut like a Norfolk jacket, a style commonly used for hunting, golfing, and walking. It was worn with a white shirt, black tie, and a wide-brimmed hat. Daisy was no longer slender, and she was a stocky little figure in her uniform. But she loved wearing it. With a knife, whistle, and rope hanging from her belt, she looked like an army general.

World War I ended on November 11, 1918, when the armistice was signed. Daisy lost no time booking passage for her home in England. Her financial affairs needed attention. She was anxious to see her English friends and hear what was going on with Girl Guides. There was much to tell them about the progress her American Girl Scouts were making. Daisy hadn't been able to go to England since the spring of 1917, when the United States entered the war.

Lady Olave Baden-Powell was now active as head of the Girl Guides in Great Britain. At a luncheon in London, the women active in Girl Guiding brought up the subject of an international organization of Girl Scouts and Girl Guides.

To Daisy, it was the most exciting idea she'd heard since B.P. had told her about the Scouts. Troops had been formed in many countries, but until now nothing had been done to bring these girls together. Daisy had always thought of Scouting as an organization not just for the girls of Savannah or the United States, but for girls everywhere. Now there would be one great big worldwide organization! She offered to help in any way she was needed.

A few months later, on February 21, 1919, Daisy attended the first International Council meeting at Girl Guide headquarters in London. She represented the Girl Scouts of the U.S.A., who now numbered forty thousand.

One of the speakers at the meeting was Anstruther Thompson, a woman whom Daisy liked very much. But when she spoke, the audience was not applauding her. Daisy said later, "I determined that I at least would show my appreciation, so, although I could not hear a word of what she was saying, I clapped and called, 'Hear! Hear!' every time she paused. It was only afterward that I found her speech had been all about me and must have sounded like this: 'Mrs. Low is a very remarkable woman.' 'Hear! Hear!' from Daisy Low. 'It is a marvelous piece of work to have founded the Girl Scouts of the United States.' Loud applause from me, while the audience remained in stony silence!"

When Daisy came back to America in May 1919, Lord and Lady Baden-Powell came with her. Proudly she took her friends to the National Headquarters to meet the Girl Scout leaders. The Baden-Powells also visited Pine Tree Camp near Plymouth, Massachusetts, a national training school for leaders.

Sir Robert made speeches to enormous crowds all over the United States and Canada. Daisy went along wherever B.P. spoke. Many questions were asked about how the organization worked in his country, and information and opinions were exchanged. Because England was a small country, a few good leaders could keep the Girl Guides running smoothly. The Girl Scouts of the U.S.A., a large, rapidly growing organization in a big country, needed trained professional workers and a paid full-time staff.

More and more workers began to get salaries. Edith Macy, chairman of the executive committee, continued as a volunteer, but Jane Deeter Rippin, a trained social worker, became the paid national director.

Daisy felt the organization was in good hands. At the National Convention in January 1920, she resigned as president, giving the job to Anne Hyde Choate. Daisy took the title of "The Founder of the Girl Scouts of the U.S.A." Later, her birthday, October 31, was made Founder's Day. It wasn't easy for Daisy to give up the reins of her precious organization. Yet she thought it was best for the girls. She enjoyed organizing troops and going to meetings, but she didn't like tending to routine details.

Also, she needed freedom to devote her time to the worldwide organization. She represented the Girl Scouts of the U.S.A. on the International Council of Girl Guides and Girl Scouts, and she attended all the international meetings, called world camps.

The first international conference was held in the summer of 1920 in Oxford, England. It was a huge success. The theme of the conference was peace and friendship. Representatives of Girl Guides and Girl Scouts from fourteen countries attended. They decided to hold a world conference every other year; the next one would be held in Cambridge, England, in 1922.

Daisy's finances had improved, so she generously paid the expenses to that conference of delegates who didn't have the money to pay their own way.

Daisy may have been busy with international affairs, but she made it her business to spend time with "her girls." She had never lost touch with the Savannah troops. Through the years she wrote to them, her letters filled with funny misspelled words. Whenever she was in Savannah, she attended meetings to get acquainted with new members, and she always took a motherly interest in the girls.

In 1922, shortly after the second world conference, or Encampment as it was now called, an American woman, Anne Archbold, gave the British Girl Guides a beautiful tract of land in New Forest, England. The site was called Foxlease. One cottage was set apart for the entertainment of Girl Guides and Girl Scouts of all nations, and it was turned over to Daisy to fix up as she pleased. She named the cottage "the Link" to symbolize the bond between the two countries she loved. Daisy gave much time and thought to the cottage's furnishings, and she painted the inside herself, decorating it with charming little medallions. The Link had the only bathtub in camp, and Daisy invited the girls to come over whenever they wished to take a bath. Each morning different girls came to bathe, and they often stayed for breakfast.

Dedicated to Daisy, the Link is a memorial in England to the woman who "had no children of her own and so devoted her great love of young people, first to her nieces and nephews and afterward to her worldwide family of Scouts and Guides."

As much as Daisy loved Foxlease, she was disappointed when it was chosen for the Third World Encampment. She had hoped the next conference would be held in the United States. When Daisy went to Foxlease for the Encampment in 1924, she found that the British Guides had carved over the door of the Link:

JULIETTE LOW

UNITED STATES   GREAT BRITAIN

Another place dear to Daisy's heart was a camp for girls and leaders on Lookout Mountain in Georgia. According to Dorris Hough, who later became the camp director, this place could only be named "Camp Juliette Low." This was because Daisy had discovered the site and had finally convinced Mr. Ledbetter, the owner of the land, to give some of his beautiful property to the Girl Scouts.

On the day the property was to be transferred to the Girl Scouts, Daisy picked up Dorris in an old rundown car. She had brought along a suitcase, four boxes, a crate of fruit, an umbrella, and a Pekinese dog. Dorris added her suitcase, and they wheezed along to the notary's office in a little town at the foot of Lookout Mountain. This was where Daisy was to sign the deed. When they finally arrived, they found that Mr. Ledbetter had sent the deed without the seal, and the deed couldn't be registered by the notary until the seal was on.

Daisy telephoned Mr. Ledbetter. Sure enough, he

had the seal—he had just forgotten to send it along with the deed. But he couldn't bring the seal down to the notary's office now because he was busy working.

Well, then, Daisy would go up the mountain and bring the deed to him.

The notary had to come along, too, to witness the signing. The poor man was pushed into the car and squeezed among the dog, various boxes, and suitcases.

Away they went up the side of the mountain, with the car bouncing, the dog yapping, and the notary shouting at Daisy about her driving. Daisy yelled back that there was no sense in hollering because she was as deaf as a post.

They had just about reached Mr. Ledbetter's when they came upon a big construction machine blocking the road.

What was Daisy going to do now?

Suddenly a voice began shouting from the top of a cliff. Dorris heard it and poked Daisy, who looked up.

"I'm up here. I got the seal all right. Can you-all get up here?" It was Mr. Ledbetter.

Daisy gave the notary a stern look and called back, "Certainly we can."

The climb was steep, and getting to the top was quite a struggle. But finally they were all there, even the dog. The seal was put on, the deed notarized, and the camp site was officially and legally transferred to Daisy Low and the Girl Scouts.

Daisy visited Camp Juliette Low several times. She

Daisy tells stories to the girls
at Camp Juliette Low.

would pitch her own tent, then canoe, hike, and cook supper with the girls over the outdoor fireplaces. During supper, she'd go around to all the tables and take part in the discussions. On one visit, she read the girls' palms. She often passed on a bit of wisdom, pretending it was somebody's fortune.

Daisy enjoyed being with the girls, and they knew she cared about them. Officially she might have been known as Juliette Low, but she was always "Miss Daisy" to her Girl Scouts. They had a special song for her written to the tune of "Dixie." When Daisy was expected at camp and her car came into view, the girls would stand in the road and sing "her song." The first verse went,

> Away down South in old Savannah
> First was raised the Girl Scout Banner,
> Daisy Low, Daisy Low, Daisy Low,
> Founder dear!

And it was only Daisy they wanted to hear tell stories at their campfires. She knew legends and ghost stories about the English and Scottish castles she had stayed in. She told many Civil War stories her father had told her and yarns about Native Americans and early Chicago she'd heard from Grandfather Kinzie. Daisy's great sense of drama made every story fascinating. She kept the audience spellbound, taking all parts and using different voices. And she always brought out the humor in her stories—even if the joke was on her. The girls loved all her stories, but the one they liked best was Daisy's favorite, too—the story about Little-Ship-Under-Full-Sail. She always saved it for last.

The love Daisy got from her girls gave her peace of mind. At last she was able to free herself from the bitter memories of her marriage and her old feelings of uselessness. She was happy now.

Chapter Seven

Daisy's Farewell

Daisy's last years were difficult. She had cancer, but people didn't talk about serious chronic illnesses in those days. She kept her disease a secret from all her family and friends, except her niece, Peggy Leigh, who was a nurse. Besides being ill, Daisy had financial troubles, partly because of business failures and partly because treating her illness cost a great deal.

In spite of poor health, Daisy kept traveling and working. Because of her special zest and spirit, she had some wonderful times, too, those last years.

In 1925, she was again aboard a ship sailing to the United States and she was thinking about her newest plan. For six years she had insisted that the World Committee choose the United States as the site of an international conference. But she still had to persuade the executive committee of the Girl Scouts of the U.S.A. So far, whenever she'd mention it to the committee, they'd put her off by saying, "That's a good project. We'll save it for the future."

Daisy didn't have much future. Although she secretly had tried a number of treatments, her cancer wasn't cured. This time she wouldn't be put off. The World Encampment must be held in America in 1926.

Jane Deeter Rippin, the national director, was used to dealing with the founder's impractical schemes. When Daisy arrived at Girl Scout Headquarters and told her she wanted to discuss a new plan, Jane smiled and invited her into her office.

Jane later told the story of how Daisy's dream had poured out of her. Daisy told Jane she wanted to have the international conference in the United States the following year. She had worked everything out. She had even checked into immigration restrictions for the foreign delegates and arranged a sailing date.

Jane was speechless. The World Encampment in America next year! Then Daisy proposed the conference be held the following May at Camp Edith Macy. And while the delegates were in the United States, she wanted them to visit Washington, Boston, Buffalo, Cincinnati, Chicago, St. Louis, and Savannah.

Camp Edith Macy! Jane couldn't believe her ears. Of all Daisy's impossible plans, this was the worst. The future Camp Macy at the moment was four hundred acres of wooded hillsides near Pleasantville, New York. It had been given to the Girl Scouts in memory of Edith Carpenter Macy, who in the early days of Girl Scouts had been chairman of the board. But the camp was still on the drawing boards. There were no roads, no buildings—not even water.

Jane asked Daisy how many people she was expecting.

"Oh, something over two or three hundred," Daisy replied.

The plan meant a lot to Daisy, Jane knew, but it couldn't work. It would take several years to get the site ready for hundreds of people. Jane had tried to let her friend down gently by suggesting that it might be better to have the Encampment in Switzerland the following summer. Then Camp Edith Macy could be used in 1928, when it would be ready for such an event.

Daisy was silent. Then she walked over and touched Jane's shoulder. If the Encampment wasn't held at Camp Edith Macy the next year, Daisy said quietly, she wouldn't live to see it held in the United States.

Startled, Jane looked into Daisy's lined face, and she suddenly saw the pain and illness there. She also saw that familiar determined look that meant Daisy had made up her mind and nobody could change it. Jane pulled herself together, told Daisy that the executive committee was meeting the following week, and invited her to attend and tell them about her plans.

At first, the committee had the same reaction as Jane had. The members told Daisy that it was a good idea to have the World Encampment in the United States, but it would be better to wait until Camp Edith Macy was a reality, and they were able to provide for their guests.

Daisy wouldn't give up. She tried persuasion,

arguments, and then compromise.

"Don't put it off," she begged. "This is the time."

The look in Daisy's eyes and the pleading note in her voice somehow made the committee vote yes. The Fourth International World Conference, the first to be held outside of England, would take place at Camp Edith Macy in May 1926.

Daisy was full of joy at the committee's decision.

Invitations were sent out to all Girl Scout and Girl Guide headquarters. Acceptances began to arrive from all over the world—from Great Britain, Egypt, Lithuania, India, Norway, France. Daisy assisted with the expenses of many delegates.

Everyone was excited about the project. Jane Deeter Rippin wrote, "Girl Scout leaders in every part of the country wrote at once offering to help in any way. And a seemingly impossible task became one which was accomplished because each person called upon gave to the best of her ability—national committee members, Girl Scout leaders, and members of our national staff alike. It was a time when Girl Scouting was welded together in spirit as never before."

Committees were formed, land was cleared, buildings were constructed. Would the camp be ready when the guests arrived?

Bad weather came, and everyone was nervous— except Daisy. She sloshed through rain and mud and poked into everything, never doubting that the deadlines would be met.

Wells were dug, but no matter how deep the men drilled, they couldn't strike water. Daisy told the committee to be patient and not to worry, that they would reach water soon. And when they finally did, everyone breathed easier.

April came, and the work continued. Now the guests were starting out from their faraway homelands. Groups of special Girl Scout leaders arrived at camp to help with last-minute preparations and to act as hostesses for the week.

On a beautiful May day, Daisy, bursting with pride and happiness, stood at the pier in New York City when the *Olympic* docked. Aboard ship were Lady Baden-Powell and fifty-six foreign delegates from twenty-nine countries. They were greeted by the mayor of New York, then there was a triumphant tour up Fifth Avenue followed by a luncheon given by the Manhattan Girl Scout Council. Daisy gave the welcoming speech.

Then Daisy sailed with the guests to Boston, where they were welcomed by the governor of Massachusetts. After returning to New York, the foreign delegates plus four hundred American delegates drove to Camp Macy in a long motorcade. Daisy and Lady Baden-Powell were in the first car.

By some miracle, the camp was ready. The buildings were completed. The Great Hall's fireplaces were finished, the cabins outfitted with cots and blankets, and the tent sites were cleared and waiting. At the very last minute, water had been piped in. It had been a close race.

As Jane Deeter Rippin wrote, "We bowed the plasterers out the back door while we welcomed our guests in at the front."

It was a lovely afternoon, sunny and mild. The long, winding road up to the camp was decorated with colorful flags of different nations. The flags were held by adult Girl Scouts, who had volunteered to help the international visitors with luggage and directions. As the delegates drove up, the air was filled with the sweet scent of apple blossoms.

That evening, the formal dedication of the camp was held in the Great Hall, where there was a faint odor of new wood and paint. Dean Russell of Teachers College at Columbia University, who was a teacher of Girl Scout training courses for leaders, spoke eloquently about Edith Carpenter Macy and her part in Girl Scouting's development. Daisy listened intently with her hearing device. A flush came to her cheeks when the Dean went on to tell the audience that he'd become involved with the Girl Scouts because of the "dauntless personality" of Juliette Low.

After his speech, the international delegates formed a line, each standing beside her country's flag. One by one, the delegates put a small bundle of twigs on the blazing fire in the huge fireplace. Each told briefly, sometimes in rhyme, about the special gifts her country offered the world.

The delegate from Austria said, "Austria brings the music of her great composers, which stirs the hearts of all the world."

The Chinese delegate said, "China brings to the world her ancient civilization, her great philosophies, and her exquisite porcelain."

The delegate from the Netherlands said, "From my country come the bulbs you plant in your gardens, Rembrandt's glorious paintings, and the great idea of world peace, conceived by Hugo Grotius."

After all the delegates had spoken, everyone sang "Taps." It had been a glorious evening.

During the week that followed, the Girl Scouts and Girl Guides camped, worked, talked, and planned together. A highlight of the conference was Sir Robert Baden-Powell's speech to the delegates. If Daisy didn't feel well, nobody knew it. She seemed filled with energy, and to be always thinking of "her girls."

Lady Olave Baden-Powell wrote of Daisy's joy at the World Encampment. "I shall never forget the hour awaiting the arrival of Sir Robert, the founder of it all. Daisy Low, Anne Choate, and I strolled along the sandy lane, the bushes swaying in the wind, and the country all ablaze with the glory of spring. How *happy* she was!"

Although the World Encampment was a personal triumph, it left Daisy ill and weak. Right afterwards, she went to visit her sister Nelly in New Jersey and collapsed at her home. She told everyone she was extremely tired, and she wrote Mabel, "I am very slow in getting well; the strain of this foreign nations camp has taken it out of me."

When she was feeling a little stronger, Daisy went

home to Savannah to see that the gates she'd made at Wellsbourne were installed in a park dedicated to the memory of her parents. In the cornerstone, she placed the tools she used in building the gates. The stone pillars in which the gates were set had a daisy carved on each column.

Daisy's pain was worse now, and to her family she seemed irritable and irrational. She planned a last trip to England. Only Dr. McGuire, who was Daisy's doctor, and his wife knew her real condition, and they sailed to England with her later in 1926. It was a sad voyage for the McGuires because they were so worried about Daisy. Then one morning she scolded them for forgetting her birthday. "I want a party and a cake with lots of daisies on it," she said.

The McGuires were glad to have something to do for Daisy. They told everyone on the ship about the party. That night at dinner her place was piled high with brightly wrapped packages. The chef carried in a magnificent three-tiered cake covered with daisies.

It didn't occur to the McGuires until the next day that Daisy's birthday wasn't until October. When they put it to her, Daisy burst out laughing. She confessed that she had fooled them into thinking it was her birthday because they were so depressed and the trip seemed so dull. She thought they all needed a good birthday party to liven things up.

In England, Daisy kept going. She felt she had a lot to do in very little time. She was with Mabel every day, but she didn't even mention her illness. Daisy went over Girl Scout international records and visited her English friends. They didn't know they were seeing her for the last time. She spent her real birthday in a sanitarium, with Peggy, her niece and confidante. She still didn't tell Mabel that she was sick.

Daisy even found strength to sculpt a bust of Grandfather Gordon, one of the founders of the Central of Georgia Railroad and a former mayor of Savannah. She planned to have it cast in bronze and given to the city of Savannah when she returned.

At last she could do no more.

Very ill now, Daisy knew she had to get home if she wanted to die in Savannah. When Daisy arrived in America in early December, she went to Nelly's home in New Jersey. There was one last thing she had to do for the Girl Scouts. She sent for the top leaders and helped them set up regional conferences to be held by Girl Scouts of neighboring countries in the western hemisphere. She hoped these conferences would strengthen friendships throughout the Americas. The idea was actually Mrs. Herbert Hoover's, but Daisy wanted to be sure the plan was set in motion.

By Christmas, although Daisy wrote everyone cheerful letters, she was resting at a hospital in Richmond, Virginia. Arthur found out how ill she was and cabled Mabel, "Daisy has only six weeks to live." Mabel and her daughter started for America at once. Nelly came from New Jersey, and Arthur and his wife, Margaret, went to

Richmond to take Daisy home.

Daisy reached Savannah with very little time to spare. She lived but ten days longer. Her suffering was made easier by having her family around her.

Messages of love poured in from all over the world. So many flowers came that Daisy said laughingly, "There won't be any left for the funeral if this keeps up."

The message she liked the best came in a telegram from Anne Hyde Choate and the National Board of the Girl Scouts. It said, "You are not only the first Girl Scout but the best Girl Scout of them all."

Juliette Gordon Low died in Savannah on Monday, January 17, 1927. According to her wishes, she was buried in her Girl Scout uniform with decorations of honor—the Silver Fish of the English Girl Guides and the jeweled Thanks Badge of the Girl Scouts of the U.S.A. Folded in the breast pocket, just as Daisy had placed it, was Anne Hyde Choate's telegram. All the Girl Scouts in Savannah formed her honor guard on the steps of Christ Church, where the funeral service was conducted. And Little-Ship-Under-Full-Sail sailed bravely from the earth.

A friend said after her death, "There is no question that the world is a much duller place since Daisy left it."

As always, even at the end of her life, Daisy's thoughts were of her girls. She'd always said it was the girls who "must come first." When people complimented her about giving something so wonderful to so many girls, she told them that Girl Scouting caught on because it was what the girls themselves wanted. "The Angel Gabriel himself couldn't have made them take it if they hadn't wanted it."

She left the Girl Scouts of Savannah most of the carriage house in back of her property where the first troop had met so long ago and where the Girl Scouts were still meeting.

One of her last acts was to add a paragraph to her will that said, "I leave and bequeath to my family my friendships especially my beloved Girl Scouts."

Few women have been honored by the United States government as Juliette "Daisy" Gordon Low has been. During World War II, a Liberty Ship of the United States Merchant Marine was named for her, and in 1948 the U.S government issued a Juliette Low postage stamp, picturing Daisy in the uniform she loved. In the 1980s, the Juliette Gordon Low Federal Office Complex was the second federal building approved by Congress to be named after a woman.

The Juliette Low World Friendship Fund was established in 1927 at the Girl Scout National Convention, to promote Girl Scouting and Girl Guiding throughout the world. The fund was started because of Daisy's interest in the international sisterhood of all Guides and Scouts. It continues to promote peace and good will between countries, as Daisy would have liked. Not only does the fund pay travel expenses for girls to attend Girl Guide and Girl Scout events all over the world, it provides monies for hygiene and sanitation training in developing countries as well as relief for disasters such as famines, floods, and earthquakes.

The Gordon house in Savannah, where Daisy was born, was purchased by the Girl Scouts of the U.S.A. in 1953 and dedicated in 1956 as an historic house museum and national program center for the Girl Scouts. It was named the "Birthplace." Troops and individuals come from all over the world to visit Daisy's birthplace.

At the time of her death there were 167,925 members in the Girl Scouts of U.S.A. In 1995, there were 3.4 million members, including girls, adult volunteers, and professional worker members from every kind of economic and racial background. Girls in 1912 could earn badges like "Flyer," "Artist," and "Telegrapher." Today, girls work toward badges in Aerospace, Prints and Graphics, and Science Around Town, which includes learning about communications satellites.

Juliette Gordon Low was a leader who helped change forever society's ideas about what women could do. Her vision did a great deal to break down the cultural restrictions placed on young girls living in the early 1900s. Berte DeSio, a woman who became a Girl Scout in 1921, put it this way, "In those days if you were a teenage girl and *not* a Girl Scout you didn't do much outside of your own neighborhood. Girl Scouting was a great adventure."

One of Daisy's "girls" had this to say about her, "This lady is a very fun person. She never makes you feel like you are dumb or silly just because you are a kid. She always has time to talk to you even if she is busy. She knows what you're talking about and she laughs at your jokes, but never at you. She makes you feel grown up when you know it's all right to be a girl because she was one herself. My mother says she is not always ladylike and I think that's good!"

Daisy's courage and spirit despite her ill health, deafness, and advancing years continues to be an inspiration to the girls of the world. Her goal, and the goal of the Girl Scout movement, was to help each girl to think big—to discover and develop the possibilities within her and in the world around her. Daisy wanted "her girls" to grow up in a friendly, peaceful world, and become independent, courageous women filled with love and laughter.

Chronology

1860   Juliette Magill Kinzie Gordon, "Daisy," is born, on October 31.

1861   *The Civil War begins.*

1864   *Savannah surrenders to Union forces.*

1865   Daisy, her mother, and her sisters visit Grandmother and Grandfather Kinzie in Chicago.

       The Civil War ends.

       President Lincoln is assassinated.

1879   Daisy begins her studies at the Mesdemoiselles Charbonniers' finishing school in New York City.

1885   Daisy becomes partially deaf in one ear.

1886   Daisy marries William "Billow" Low on December 21. She becomes totally deaf in her other ear.

1889   Billow purchases Wellesbourne House in Warwickshire, England.

1898   *The Spanish-American War begins.*

       Spain surrenders, and the Spanish-American War ends.

1901   *Queen Victoria of Great Britain dies; her eldest son becomes King Edward VII.*

1905   William Low dies.

1908   *Scouting for Boys,* by Sir Robert Baden-Powell, is published.

1911   Daisy meets Sir Robert Baden-Powell.

Daisy organizes a Girl Guide patrol in Glen Lyon, Scotland.

1912 Margaret "Daisy Doots" Gordon is registered as the first Girl Guide in the United States, on March 12.

1913 The name of the United States organization is changed from "Girl Guides" to "Girl Scouts."
The handbook *How Girls Can Help Their Country* is published.
Girl Scout National Headquarters is established in the Munsey Building in Washington, D.C.

1914 *World War I begins.*
The Panama Canal opens.

1915 The First Girl Scout Convention is held, in Washington, D.C., and the First National Council meeting is held.
Daisy is elected president.

1917 *The United States enters World War I.*
Girl Scouts help in the war effort

1918 *World War I ends.*

1919 Daisy attends the first meeting of the International Council of Girl Guides and Girl Scouts in London, England.

1920 Daisy resigns as president and takes the title of Founder of the Girl Scouts.
The First International Conference of Girl Guides and Girl Scouts is held in Oxford, England.

1926 The Fourth International Conference is held at Camp Edith Macy, Pleasantville, New York.

1927 Daisy dies in Savannah, Georgia, on January 17.

Index

Boldface page numbers indicate illustrations.
Roman numerals indicate page numbers of the photo insert.